# MOTORCYCLES, LIFE AND...

Road Dog Publications was formed in 2010 as an imprint of Lost Classics Book Company and is dedicated to publishing the best in books on motorcycling for the thoughtful rider. We are pleased to produce this first book by Brent Allen and introduce to the motorcycling public yet another side of this multi-talented rider and instructor.

*There are a few references to Internet URLs in the text. Road Dog Publications does not own or control the content of these sites. The Internet is continually changing and Road Dog Publications makes no guarantees that these sites referenced still exist or will remain in the same location. They are included solely as useful references for the reader. If a URL has changed, the same resource can usually be located easily by means of using one of the many search engines available.*

Motorcycles, Life, and...
© January 2011, Brent Allen, All Rights Reserved.

ISBN 978-1-890623-36-4
Library of Congress Control Number: 2011920565

An Imprint of Lost Classics Book Company

This book also available in e-book format at online booksellers. ISBN 978-1-890623-37-1

# Motorcycles, Life and...

## By Brent Allen
aka
"Captain Crash"

Publisher
Lake Wales, Florida

# ABOUT THE AUTHOR

Brent "Crash" Allen grew up in the San Francisco Bay area, graduating high school in 1981, the same year he bought his first motorcycle—a 1978 Honda XL500S. Receiving his motorcycle endorsement that year, he has kept it current ever since.

Trained and certified as an Idaho State Motorcycle Safety Instructor in April 2003, "Crash" teaches both basic and advanced motorcycling classes. He was awarded the Shining Star award by Idaho STAR in 2004 and an Award of Merit in 2010.

"Captain Crash" is well-known in the motorcycling community, having produced the popular series of motorcycle safety videos titled "Howzit Done?" which have received over a half-million views on YouTube.

The author has owned sportbikes, standards, dual sports, a motard, and now a cruiser. An equal opportunity rider—if it's got two wheels, he'll ride it.

Early on, Brent worked as a truck driver, equipment operator, light duty mechanic, pump jockey, and a freight handler. He attended college at Foothills College, Santa Monica College, and eventually Brigham Young University, where he is pursuing a degree in Mass Communications. He will finish his studies in spring of 2011. Brent went to work in broadcasting in the Salt Lake City area in 1986. He moved to Idaho in 1990, where he worked as a television photojournalist, production and operations manager, and producer/director. Brent has worked on nationally broadcast football and rodeo events as a camera operator since 1986.

In 2002, Brent was hired as a Professional Technical Educator and now teaches broadcasting to high school students. In 2005 he was voted "Teacher of the Year" by his high school teaching peers. His students have been the SkillsUSA Idaho State Champions in Television (video) Production from 2005 through 2010, SkillsUSA National Champions in Television (video) Production in 2009, and SkillsUSA Idaho State Champions in Broadcast News in 2006 and 2009.

Brent is also Fire Commissioner for the Nampa Fire Protection District and is proud to be helping first responders do their jobs and do them well.

# FOREWORD

I started teaching high school when I was thirty-seven and frankly it was a bit of "why not?" Before I found myself teaching I had done a lot of things; I'm kind of a "Sure. I'll try that. Hold my drink." kind of guy. I have picked pineapples, drove dump trucks and semis, worked as pump jockey and light duty mechanic, busted out trailers on a freight dock, worked in the TV studio, worked as a freelance camera operator at nationally televised sporting events, shot news for local TV, produced and directed some wonderfully bad local TV spots and just about anything that seemed interesting. In 2001 a friend said to me, "You're really good at this broadcasting thing, have you ever considered teaching it?" He was the "Chief Educational Officer" (read: principal) at the local high school and to make a long story short—I gave it a whirl, and it has turned out well. We've got kids who have gone on to college, technical school, and military service; our program has won multiple state championships and a national championship.

It turns out, when it comes to teaching, I don't suck. Nobody is more surprised than I.

In the spirit of total frankness, I have to let you know that

when I started teaching it was the first time in my life that I felt
my parents were really, truly proud of what I was doing. My
Grandpa Hansen was a teacher. I had never felt any weight from
that legacy, yet once I was teaching, I suddenly sensed pride from
my mother, her sisters, and her brother. I had picked up a bit of
the family torch.

My ability to teach may be biological—I don't know. But I do
know this: if I am anything of a teacher it's because of my pop.
My pop was an engineer, but what he really did well was teach.
Show him a problem, and he'd helped *you* solve it. He taught me
to stop and think a minute, to turn something over in your hand
and ask: "What does that look like?" or "What does it want to
be?" and "How can I apply this idea to that problem?"

That idea, the idea that the answer to one problem might
come from somewhere else, is paramount to my world view.
When my father was managing a research and development lab
he was responsible for hiring engineers. These were *electrical*
engineers. His favorite question to ask went like this—He would
show them a picture or a model of Mount Rushmore, then ask:
"How do you do that?" If they asked, "What?" he would ask,
"How would you build Mount Rushmore?" Hewn right out of
the mountain, perfect to scale and shape, formed perfectly—
"How would *you* make Mount Rushmore? Just run up with a
jackhammer and start hacking?" It was a mystery to me, but I'm
not an engineer of *any* kind. I couldn't posit a guess.

Pop actually taught me through it. He let me discover that
I could figure it out with a little help, that inside me was the
answer and it just needed a path out. (Look up how to build
Mount Rushmore sometime—it's pretty obvious once you think
about it.)

From the first "Motorcycles, Life and..." article people have
asked if I've got a book out somewhere. No, I said, I write these
little observational things and...what are they? Metaphoric
mayhem? Besides books are big arduous things that require
thinking and drinking and sweating; some I don't do anymore
and at others I'm not that good.

When Mike Fitterling contacted me and said, "Hey, I think you've got a book here," I was overwhelmed. I just write little pieces that tie motorcycles and life and stuff together. Grown-up me thought, "A book?" Then sixteen year old me spoke up: "Sure. Why not? Here, hold my drink." I won't lie to you, Mike is the finish guy. He got things in order, organized the ideas, did the formatting, and with his knowledge of the ins-and-outs we got to press—no Mike, no book.

In the end, what we have is a collection of times when I realized that the answers to some of life's problems are clearly modeled in motorcycling. Times when I said to broadcasting students, "It's just like when you're riding a motorcycle," and...presto!—story and metaphor. It's that simple sometimes.

I remember one day, when I was eighteen and I was riding my Honda XL500 to work when I realized my dad was driving the car behind me. Stopped at a four way, I proceeded down a long, tree lined, quiet, residential street. I lollygagged and let Pop get right behind me, then I whacked it wide open and hung out a long second-gear-on-the-balance-point wheelie. After work, at home, I waited for my pop to say something. More patient than I, he outlasted me.

"Whaddaya think of that wheelie this morning?" I asked.

"Pretty neat," he said, "pretty neat."

My father passed away on New Year's Day, 2007, after a long fight with heart disease. There are many times I wish I could still turn to him and ask, "Whaddaya think? I think this is a book. Pop? Whaddaya think?"

# TABLE OF CONTENTS

# My Dad

Our experiences shape who we are as motorcyclists. We are the sum of our experiences. Every ride adds to who we are and can change the way we look at the world. My first cognizant motorcycling memory is from inside the family car. I was about eight years old and we were at the intersection of El Camino Real and Grant Road. Three guys on two-stroke enduros were crossing through the intersection perpendicular to us. All three popped the front up and wheelied through the intersection. It was the coolest thing I had ever seen. I can't tell you what kind of bikes they were, or if the guys were wearing helmets, or even where we were going! I just remember thinking, "That is the coolest thing I have ever seen."

(In fact today, when I ride up to a minivan, and I see kids popping their heads up to look at me on the bike, my first instinct is to look around and see if I can sneak a wheelie in—but that's another story.)

Not long after that my big brothers' friends started getting bikes. My brother Jeff's friend, James, got a Honda 185; the first motorcycle on which I was given a ride. James's twin brother, Bill, got an Yamaha RD400 which thrilled and scared me to death

1

as it screamed up the street, once or twice with me clinging to the back. Then another friend got a red Yamaha XS750, and eventually, a cool color matched windjammer which was the platform for my longest passenger ride.

That "looking" as a eight year-old transformed into a fascination that led me to ask for a ride whenever I thought I could pull it off. Little brothers have and continue to not be cool—but asking for a ride was one thing I could do that wasn't met with contempt.

By the time I was a senior in high school I was working after school and weekends with one simple goal: get a bike. So I worked. And saved. And my parents said, "No, you're not." So I worked, and I saved some more. I needed transportation, so I bought a beater BMW 1600 sedan, drove that into the ground, sold it for parts, got more than I paid for it, and decided it was time.

Two important things had happened. First I had turned eighteen. Second, my parents had been saddled with a Beemer 1600 up on blocks in the driveway that slowly, part by part, disappeared. I sold the carcass in one piece—boy, were they glad to see it go. That lingering death of the Beemer created a window of opportunity. A motorcycle takes up *much* less space. Scavengers don't show up and take one headlight then leave dangling wires from an empty socket and second, you can wheel a motorcycle back behind the garage, and no one knows it's there.

So I watched the want ads, talked to my friends at work, and found a 1978 Honda XL500S that was the right price.

Mind you I had ridden *on* motorcycles but never *operated* one. But I'd bought a Bell MotoStar helmet, and had a denim jacket and leather gloves, so I was good to go. I copped a ride on the back of a friend's Yamaha XT500, then another on a Honda XL185, and headed to Cupertino and did the deal. The transaction was notable for its brevity. I handed the guy the money, he handed me the pink slip, and suddenly I was standing there owning a motorcycle.

Sitting on it was no problem. Riding it? I've always held that the good Lord didn't want me to go hungry so he gave me mechanical skill. I was eighteen. I could operate anything mechanical. I had graduated high school with a Class 1 operators license, I was a licensed truck driver, I could operate forklifts and front loaders—if it was a machine—I could make it work.

So I wasn't smart enough to be frightened. I got the "this is the clutch—this is the throttle—this is the brake—this is the shifter" speech, put on the helmet and gloves, and got this final word of advice:

"Just follow us and do what we do. Do *exactly* what we do."

OK. How hard could that be? We saddled up and took off. A lot has been written about rider training. There are volumes on how to learn to ride. The Motorcycle Safety Foundation has a great training course, as does Team Oregon and Idaho Star. It all starts with a classroom and then range time, coaching and evaluation, practice and refinement.

It turned out that on the way home there was a certain terrain feature I was unaware of: railroad tracks; a raised crossing, something that today I could call "a ramp." I followed. And when they accelerated, I accelerated; and when they stood up, I stood up. They stayed on the throttle, and I stayed on the throttle. They flew, and I flew. They landed, and I landed.

And everything was OK. I rode my first motorcycle and jumped it, too. I learned to ride the old-school way; the way most people still do: "Just follow us and do what we do and everything is gonna be OK." Isn't that the nature of life? In some things we get formalized, curriculum driven instruction; in others we just try to do what the guy in front of us did.

Today is Father's Day. This is the second one on which I can't call my dad and wish him Happy Father's Day. He's gone; but as I travel down this road of life I can still see his taillight out there in front of me. I remember how he treated me. I remember how, once I embraced riding, he supported me, warned me of danger, made sure I had good insurance, and reminded me to be safe. I remember how much he cared about everything I did.

I never knew how much time he spent awake at night worried about me. I know it now because I lie in bed and worry about my kids. Now, as my oldest son gets ready to leave for college, I worry if I can do this right. How can I make sure I'm doing and saying the right things? The answer is simple: I just do what Dad did. Dad loved me; I love my kids. Dad wanted me to get the most I could out of life. I want success for my kids. Dad stopped and waited for me, made sure I got there safe, encouraged me and led me forward again.

He's out there now, just ahead of me, waiting for me to catch up, watching me be the man he was, teaching my son to be all the man he can be.

Thanks Pop.

# GREAT EXPECTATIONS

What are you looking for? What are your expectations? I expect to be taxed—continually. I expect to be taxed when I die—well, not me directly but my family if I have enough assets. Some taxes are called fees, but they're taxes anyway you cut them. I pay fees to register all my motorized stuff.

But enough whining about giving money to "The Man."

What are your expectations? A quick peek at the word *expect* gives some insight. First, it's a verb. Second, it can mean different things. It can mean you have an expectation that something will happen—like I expect to retire someday. How? I'm not sure. It can also mean you have some reason to expect to have something happen. You go to the burger joint and you *expect* to be able to get a burger. Sitting at home *hoping* a burger shows up is silly.

I am particularly taken with the idea you should have a reasoned expectation for something. As you might know I work at a high school. Kids expect a lot of stuff. See, for me the mark of maturity is the difference between explanation 1 and explanation 2. Kids just expect things to happen because they *want* it to—they have no reason *why* it should. It's not a reasonable expectation—they just hope it does.

Lots of teens I know "expect" to get Division 1 collegiate athletic scholarships. They expect to become famous rap stars. Or they expect they'll become movie stars. Most of these expectations are based on raw, unsubstantiated hope. They just want to be rappers, stars, or athletes and one of the benevolent lies we tell is that "If you want it bad enough—you can do it!" Which is a bit of a whopper, because you also need talent and some luck to become a star. Tupac Shakur, who teens will point to as "coming up the hard way" actually attended a Baltimore performing arts high school and performed Shakespeare, studied poetry, and was the Mouse King in the Nutcracker. It's easy to forget that paying your dues is...well, paying your dues. Tupac was a background dancer for the Digital Underground (the Humpty Hump guys) before he got his break.

Teens at my school just expect they'll automatically become famous because they want to be famous. There's no rational basis for their expectations—they just hope it enough that they expect it'll happen. I was in the counselors' office the other day and a young man was trying to weasel out of a class he didn't like. The counselor wouldn't let him because if he dropped, then an automatic F attached itself to this kid's transcript. (I was there just for a moment, dropping in to ask a quick question, when I witnessed this). I had listened for a moment when the student blithely told the counselor that academics wasn't a big deal, and I decided to stick my nose in.

"Can I ask a question?" I asked the counselor.

"Sure!" said the counselor.

"You mind if I ask you a question?" I directly asked the student.

"Yeah, shoot," He said.

"Are you going on to college or tech school—after you graduate I mean?"

"Yes." He looked me straight in the eye and added, "I'm going on a football scholarship."

"Where?" See, "Where?"—that's the kind of question that can stop an expectation in its tracks—it's a reality question.

He looked at me kind of like I was stupid. Didn't I know?— Somewhere!

"Well," I said, "you're a Junior, right? (He nods) And if you're a scholarship candidate then you're going to be an All State Selection this year—right? All Conference Defensive First Team kind of stuff? You know the stuff that gets you noticed and looks good on your resume? *And if you're gonna get a full ride athletic scholarship* somewhere—they're gonna be scouting you right now! They'll have at least made some kind of contact with your coach, and he'll be sending them your stats and that kind of thing. So, my question is: what schools are scouting you?"

Dumb look, mute kid, surprise!

No schools are even aware this kid exists. Why? 'Cause he's just another decent high school football player. They're not going to be offering him any money because they don't waste time and energy on someone who—in the long run—is gonna be on the Scout Team and spend his time getting thrashed *for free.* Best case scenario?—an invite to walk on. He's an average high school defensive lineman—which means size wise he's a small NCAA D1 linebacker. Skill wise? Well...

Even after throwing water on his dream and trying to explain that his academic record will be *very* important to a school considering courting him, when I left he *still* expects a full ride Division 1 scholarship. But he's not looking for it with "reason or justification." He just wants it to happen; to make it happen he has a lot of work to do and a lot of luck needs to come into play. I'm not saying he's not a scholarship kid; I'm just saying he's got to get on the job and start paying the dues. Time to study Shakespeare and do some background dancing.

Here's our motorcycle tie in: What do you expect from motorcycling? Riding has been a fast growing share of the transportation market. There are more riders every ding dang day. What do they expect?

Good gas mileage—what's a reasonable expectation there? 100mpg? 50mpg? 40mpg? This is one of those places where we need to temper our expectations. A 1000cc sportbike or a 1800cc cruiser are both gonna be lucky to break 40mpg. Large displacement motorcycles just don't get monstrously good gas mileage. If you're riding an 1800cc bike then you have more displacement than a Toyota Yaris—so don't be surprised if you get equivalent mileage (35mpg). Feeding that beast takes gas. Turn that throttle hard and that thing gulps big fuel. If you expect to get great money-saving mileage then be reasonable and buy something under 600ccs.

Do you expect ease of parking? Well, heck, you'll get that. There are loads of trick little places you can squeeze your bike into—just be reasonable and remember: *no reverse*. You squeeze in and you've got to back paddle out! Another parking drawback? Local laws! You may fit, but that doesn't mean you're legal. Check for local codes on things like distances from doorways and sidewalk clearances! Personally, I've never received a ticket for my crazy parking antics but never say never...

Do you expect protection from the elements? Air conditioning in the summer? Rain in your face? Are you figuring on hauling groceries? Or passengers?

What do you expect? What's justified and reasonable? It's a fair question and a question you should ask before you begin your riding career—it's a fair question to ask before you buy a new bike, new gear, or even just go for a ride.

Are your expectations reasonable and justified?

What are my motorcycling expectations? I expect to see beautiful scenery. I expect to meet new people and have camaraderie with fellow riders. I expect to worry about fuel on long rides because of limited fuel capacity. I expect to stop and get good grub at small local diners. I expect to be unable to carry anything of consequence (unless I wear my backpack). I expect to be a little hot sometimes, a little cold others, and just right the majority of the time. I expect to be dry most of the time and quite possibly wet occasionally. I expect cars won't always see me, and I'll have to avoid them once in a while. I expect I may fall, so I wear a helmet. I expect to save some gas and trade it for some comfort.

What's my *biggest* expectation? I expect I'll have fun riding my motorcycle; and *that* is a justified and reasonable expectation.

# MENUS

I love menus. A menu is like a world of possibilities. Recently I was at place in Kansas City called "Mama's 39th Street Diner." You want to see a menu? They got a menu. Good chow. Loads of good chow. They have a cake display up front that knocks you out—made myself sick on carrot cake, but it was worth it.

I like to read menus. I like to make stupid decisions with menus. You know, that "this sounds weird, but probably tastes good" kind of thing. I ate my way through Kansas City (thank you Food Channel, NCgal, and crew!). We stopped at a place called "Grinders," and I saw something that looked good in that weird way. It was a "Goldberg" pizza—crust, pesto, olive oil, salmon and cream cheese; yes a pizza with pesto, salmon, and cream cheese. As Yoda would say "Great it was!"

When you're at a new eatery what do you order? Do you go out on a limb and try something new? Do you look to see if a "hamburger" is on the menu? Do you just say, "I'm not ready yet," let someone else order and say, "I'll have that too!" I admit, I've done the lazy, easy "follow the leader" thing and let someone else make the decision and then just followed.

Sometimes it works out—sometimes it don't.

I was in my car the other day, and I was getting off the freeway. I was just following the car in front of me (bad plan, wasn't looking ahead at all, just lazy). At the bottom of the ramp he stopped. I stopped. He put on his left turn signal. I put on my left turn signal. The car behind me put on their left turn signal. The light changed to green left arrow; the guy in front turned left, went in way too shallow, and had to really cut it hard to stay in the lane, I went in really shallow and had to really cut it hard to stay in the lane; and the guy behind me did the same thing.

I know because I looked in the mirror. See, once I realized I had blindly followed the guy in front of me, and screwed up, I looked to see if the guy behind me had followed me. He had! So did the guy behind him.

Following blindly isn't always a good idea. At the core of motorcycling is a single track vehicle with an internal combustion engine—that's what motorcycles are! There are different brands of motorcycles and different styles of motorcycles, but fundamentally they are all the same, two wheels and an internal combustion engine. That doesn't make them identical, it just makes for a wide palette. It's like food! Food is food right? It's all the same? *Wrong!* You'll find tremendous variations on food. You can get food just about anywhere. Go into a bar; you can get food. Go into a deli; you can get food. Go to a gas station; food. But what kind? That's what menus are for—to tell you what kind of food is available.

If you're in a pizza joint, don't be surprised if they don't have raw fish. If you wanted sashimi you should be at a sushi bar *not* a pizza joint. If you want breakfast at 10pm at night, the piano bar at the Waldorf probably ain't serving! Want a good hoagie? Don't go to barbeque joint.

The type of restaurant is the first part of the menu. Want a motorcycle? Don't go to the Chevy dealer. Want a cruiser, then you need to go to a dealer that serves cruisers. Want to hit that triple and take a nice shot off the berm? Find a dealer with dirtbikes. If you want to go across the country and never put a wheel on asphalt, then you need to go to a dealer that sells adventure touring bikes and reeeeeally good GPSs.

A big chunk of this really comes down to you. Why do you want a bike? What do you want it to do? I was the instructor in a training class once, and this kindly older lady was in the class. As a passenger she had really enjoyed *riding on* motorcycles. This was her chance to learn to *ride* motorcycles. About half way through the course she realized that she liked *riding on* motorcycles but didn't enjoy *riding* motorcycles. It was impressive to see that she had come to understand that she was a passenger, not an operator. Fortunately she hadn't purchased a bike yet. Can you imagine plunking 12K down for a new ride, getting on it for a week, and then realizing you don't like to ride?! Better to find out before you purchase.

First: go places that are new to you. Give new stuff a chance! When I'm at a restaurant that's new to me, and they have neat stuff on the menu the first thing I do is look for a "sampler" plate; that way you can order something that will give everyone at the table a taste of what's available. MSF, Team Oregon, IdahoSTAR classes are a great way of sampling motorcycling. You pay your money, they supply the bike, the range, helmets, instructors— the whole enchilada. All you need to do is show up dressed appropriately. Riding someone else's bike to see if you like riding is a good deal. Getting some professional training and input? Good deal.

Second, remember that motorcycling is a broad palette. There are more specialized machines available to motorcyclists than any other motor enthusiasts. One problem we face as riders is that once we've picked a flavor, we never try anything else. We just come in and order the same thing day after day after day. Or we follow the guy in front of us who has the same thing day after day after day.

May I suggest something?

Ride another flavor bike. Try a new road. Experiment a little. What's the worst that can happen? You might find out you can ride with your feet in front of you! Or that windshields are really neat! Or that the trip around the lake is better clockwise than counterclockwise! Maybe riding in the high desert is more fun than you realize—or you could learn that a 300 mile day can be pretty dang cool on the right bike, especially if you know where to stop and eat.

If someone offers you a taste of a pesto/salmon/cream cheese pizza, take a bite. Part of what divides the motorcycle nation is that we order what the guy next to us is ordering. Isn't it time to look over at the next table and say, "I'll have what they're having"? Come on, take a chance—you might like it. The worst thing that can happen is you'll know another thing you don't like!

# FIRST KISSES

Remember your first kiss? I do. Well, not *yours*, but I remember *mine*. Unless, of course, you're that one special girl who is the first girl I kissed. If it was you then you remember being out behind the woodshop, with the smell of sawdust in the air...the awkward embrace, the moment of trying to figure out "go right or go left"... ahhhh youth. First kisses are fun!

Nice thing is you get more than one. There's that original, very first, "never-been-kissed" kiss and then later a first kiss with a new somebody. (If you're married to the first person you ever kissed, trust me, I'm impressed and you are an *extreme* exception). I've been kissing the same girl for over 20 years now. (Don't tell her but when we had our first kiss? It wasn't my first!) I still get butterflies when we kiss but the worry that I may throw up on her when I pull the trigger and lean in, is, well, gone. Sometimes I'm thinking, this might not work, and I worry about her turning her head and giving me a cheek but that's about the worst thing that can happen now. (Yeah, I still get a thrill from kissing Mrs. Crash.)

That said, let's talk bikes! Ever buy a new ride—or a "new to you" one? Remember throwing your leg over the first time?

13

The thrill and the fear? The first time you were going to ride for yourself? The first time you decided to unleash the cat and turn that throttle wide open? Recall that first busy freeway trip? Or that time you finally went for it into that last turn heading back to the barn?

I'm not talking about the first time a car pulled out of a driveway in front of you, or the first time the light went green and you were slipping it into an intersection when you realized *that* car, the one coming from the right, wasn't going to stop. Or that there was diesel or antifreeze on the road in front of you. This won't be a discussion of unfortunate pucker moments, the times when fortune fails and disaster looms; this is a discussion of "pucker up" moments; the moments where you "screw your courage to the sticking place" and just-go-for-it. Like your first kiss, or first big purchase, or first ride, or first wheelie.

Did he just say "first wheelie"?

Yes, yes I did. (Shocked gasp).

Oh come on, set that teacup down and don't stick your pinkie out when you drink. We're grown-ups here. I know not everybody wheelies, or stoppies, or does a smoky burnout, *but* there is a reason they do. It's the same reason you went for that first kiss—because it feels good, and it was dangerous, and it could end in glory or disaster; hero or zero...it was thrilling. If you're sitting there worrying and saying to yourself, "But Crash, I've never wanted to do a wheelie!" That's OK. Think about your first kiss. In life, like in motorcycles, every once in a while you have to *go for it*. You have to stop thinking, pondering, and pausing and simply pull the trigger.

You've seen that person; you've *been* that person that sits there with their finger on the trigger and just can't seem to pull it. Sweat starts up in your hair line, your heart beats faster; the world sounds muffled as you hear the rush of blood flowing through your ears. What happens if you do? You'll be in debt for 36 months *or* the bike could come over on top of you *or* you could get a ticket *or* she might say "yes" and you'll actually have to go out on a date (and be charming and interesting and polite for 3 hours! Yikes!) *or* you'll have strapped on a 30 year mortgage *or* move to a new city *or* swear to protect the constitution *or* just insert your personal fear here.

Big things require big chances. Big chances require big...ahhh... commitment. Yeah sometimes you have to suck it up, suppress your fear, trust your gut, stick to your plan and GO FOR IT.

What do you want to hear about? First wheelie or first kiss? (This is one of those pull the trigger moments...ahhhh...errrrr... OK!)

Since both happened within a couple of years of each other lets go chronologically—*backward!* It's 1981. I turned eighteen and cash in hand bought a '78 Honda XL500S. It had a 23 inch front wheel, looked like some kind of weird speedway bike, and was red. I bought it at the end of my senior year in high school. I was eighteen, had a great job driving dump trucks and delivering landscaping supplies *and* had friends who were willing to teach me to ride so it just happened naturally. In retrospect, I probably paid too much for the bike but, dang it, I wanted to do it and all I could think of was pulling the trigger. So I did.

Often on my way home I would pass by one of the cheerleader's home. She lived on the same street as my friend Tom. If you remember what it's like being eighteen, with your first motorcycle, and in proximity of an attractive young lady then you know what I was feeling. Naw, you can *guess* what I was feeling. One day, as I was leaving Tom's house I decided it was time to pull my first wheelie. I clearly remember that tight chested feeling as I whacked that thing wide open and the front came up.

And up.

And up.

And OVER!

Followed by the usual: road, sky, road, *then* cheerleader's house, sky, road, cheerleader's house, sky. An accident of this sort can be very damaging. You can break bones, smash sensitive parts, sever synapses, and generally bust yourself up. In my case, I deeply, deeply bruised my ego; got the opportunity to learn how to replace handlebars, fenders, and taillights; and changed my route from Tom's house to my house. It was a learning experience.

Do I regret pulling that trigger? Nope. Did I come off lucky? Heck yeah. But I'm not going to curse luck or dwell on what may have been. I pulled the trigger, dodged my own bullet, and lived to learn from it. However, today we're not talking about bad consequences from pulling that trigger, we're talking about the "girding up your loins," "setting your teeth" and *doing* something— even if there's attached risk.

The idea of pulling the trigger in a situation of complete safety, of absence of risk, is asinine. If there's no risk—why hesitate? Complete safety makes for easy decision making. Is Mrs. Crash *always* going to kiss me back? Nope. Every once in a while I get the cheek. Why? I don't always know—sometimes I know what I did, maybe I don't. Sometimes I think I deserved that. Don't become confused here, kissing Mrs. Crash is exciting every time because I get a cheap thrill from that "look what I can do—I cannot believe this, I'm the luckiest guy in the world! This woman loves me!" but in the back of my mind, faintly speaks a voice that says: "Hope this works!"

Here's the story of my first ever kiss. I was fifteen; it was behind the woodshop at the high school. I was on my first "official" date, which happened to be attending a play my friend, Tom, was in. Somehow, afterwards I wound up out behind the shop with a wonderful, pretty girl who clearly wanted me to kiss her. I was scared. I never had kissed anyone before, had no technique, no idea what I was doing. It was awkward and frightening and embarrassing. I clearly didn't know what I was doing but was having a good time failing. Here's the kicker; she stops, looks me right in the eye, and says: "Just open your mouth stupid!"

Got it; you don't have to tell me twice.

True story: I can still wheelie. I'm not a wheelie god by any means. If I'm lucky I can get up on the balance point and kick it up a gear; *and* all my wheelies are in parking lots. With one notable exception:

One day, somehow, I wound up riding home right in front of

the lovely Mrs. Crash. She was behind me in her car, and we were on a long straight road. To be honest, we live in farm country and out here it's a half to one mile between intersections. We just left an intersection, and I thought—should I? There's a pretty girl right there behind me watching!

I could hear the blood rushing through my head, my chest got tight—and I thought how embarrassing would it be to loop a wheelie showing off for my wife and then get run over by her when I looped it. Things like "you're over forty years old" and "what if you get a ticket" and "you don't heal up near as fast as you did" were running through my head. Mrs. Crash was probably wondering why I was going twenty miles per hour in a fifty zone and I....just....pulled the trigger.

The front came up, my right foot was securely hovering over the rear brake in case it got too high, and I brought it up in second, snicked third, and bounced it on the balance point with the throttle. I just hung it out. Let's just say as I realized we were coming up to another intersection I put it back down.

At home I was taking off my gear in the shop as Mrs. Crash walked in and said, "That was a long one. What was that for?"

"For you," I answered, and I went for the kiss. Yeah, low risk, but you'd be a knucklehead if you didn't try.

If there's no first wheelie—there's never a second. If there's not a first kiss, there can't be a reprise. Whatever that thing is, cowboy up and pull the trigger, trust me, it's worth it.

# SWATHING

Have you ever mowed hay? I mean swath it? Gone out to eight or ten or 100 acres of lush, thick, green alfalfa and cut that sucker down and laid it out in windrows? It's cool as heck. Here's how it works: you get a swather, which is a big fricking self propelled sickle bar cutter with an engine, cab, and header. The header is where the sickle bar is—it's between twelve and twenty feet wide—your swath is twelve to twenty *feet* wide. Yeah, that old Toro you're so proud of? The one with the 24 inch deck? This can be up to *ten times* as wide. As the hay is cut, it's swept back by a rake and up onto a set of conveyers that run it into the center of the header and roll it out the back in a windrow.

So, basically, you cut a swath of hay twenty feet wide and it leaves a three foot wide, two foot high windrow. If you've mowed, you know what I'm talking about, you're an engine of construction and destruction. You're cutting huge amounts of green, cutting it off *low*—a couple of inches off the ground. It goes from two feet to four inches and you chew it up and spit it out in clean straight row. All this leafy green growth just disappears as you go over it... it's...magical.

If you get the chance to mow—*take it*. You'll be amazed at how powerful it makes you feel. Useful, because what you're cutting will dry and be baled, up to two tons an acre. You just feel so damned cool. You mow hay just like you would a lawn; twice around the outside and then you drop in and start going up and down the field.

The first pass around the field you're a little nervous, but that fades with the second. Going around the second time you start to get your groove and you're thinking, "Is anyone looking? I mean, look at what I'm doing! My rows are straight, I'm cutting it low. Look at me! Loud, powerful, getting it done; one man against nature, in control of the elements and the machine, master of the field. Lord, Master and Commander—Fear me? FEAR THIS!"

You're the coolest guy in the world and you start to go up and down the field, up and down. And suddenly after four or five rows, it's the most boring thing you've ever done in your life. Up the field... turn around...down the field...turn around. It's loud. Your teeth rattle. The air conditioning in the cab doesn't work. The radio only gets AM, and you've already heard this particular Dr. Laura, and yes, have your wife drive the baby sitter home...blah, blah.

Mowing is a good example of *the need to know what you are getting yourself into.*

That goes double for motorcycles. Buying one? Want the loud one? Or the fast one? Or the coooool one? What's that bad boy gonna feel like on the fourth or fourteenth or fortieth time up and down the field. After 100 miles? 200 Miles? Or how about after an hour just running down that straight shot of slab between you and the next city over? How does it do in that tight spot on campus? Can you turn it around in your driveway? Do you need to be able to? Can you carry groceries? A rain coat? Lunch? Anything larger than a paperback (and I mean a short one at that)? How big a gas tank does it have—can you get there from here?

That's the problem with something that *looks* really, really cool: it is...for a while; or in the right context. It doesn't matter if it's a motorcycle, mustache, or man cave—be sure it's what you really want before you invest in something you're gonna regret.

# PERFECTION

Amongst the many, many things I do, I am a motorcycle instructor; I get to teach people how to ride motorcycles. Sounds fun? It is fun. You get to coach highly motivated people to do something that you personally love. Plus you get to deal with all sorts of people—there's not just *one* kind of person that wants to ride a motorcycle—there's *all* kinds. Again, they all *want* to learn to ride, sure some are just "taking the class to get a license" but my friends, a student that is facing what they feel is a high stakes test feels like they have a lot to lose, and they will absolutely put their back into learning. A goal is a good thing to have; it gives direction, hope, and vision to the goal setter.

The other day, for example, I had a lady in our Basic Rider Training who was highly motivated. Her husband had purchased a motorcycle for her, and she was going through the training to get her license. As we were briefing the class out on the riding range, the first question she had was: "You're going to test us, right?" Tough question; combined with the look in her eyes I could tell that the TEST was a matter of real concern to her. I never call the TEST a test. For me it is what its designation calls it: A Skills Evaluation. People really get inside their own heads and trip themselves up when they get in the TEST mode. Yes, if you come up short on the evaluation, you won't get a license waiver; but it's not the end of the world. Don't put extra pressure on yourself by focusing on the evaluation at the end of the day.

After some talking and cajoling I thought I had settled her jitters, and we started instruction. As we started to operate the bikes it became obvious that she was extraordinarily nervous. I worried we were approaching "freaked out" on the mental anxiety meter. Once a person is caught in that cascade of "I can't," things can go from bad to wretched in a matter of minutes. Pulling her from the exercise (an action that can exacerbate a problem) I stopped her next to me and this is what I said: "Take a big deep breath—I mean fill your lungs and then let it all out; you know that 'cleansing breath' thing."

She did. I said, "Feel better?" She nodded yes. I sent her back out, and she keeps riding—poorly. It was clear that she was in the deep water and foundering. Getting underway wasn't much of an issue but it was throttle control that was killing her; on and off, on and off—basically she couldn't hold a steady throttle. This sort of thing is a self-inducing problem because when she popped the throttle (abruptly opened) the bike lurched and that scares her, she then chopped the throttle (abruptly closed) and the bike pitched forward and slowed, frightening her into thinking it was stopping so she popped the throttle again which caused the bike to lurch...and so it went.

In case you've never been on a range with new riders let me set it up this way: you've got between eight and twelve raw rookies, all potentially new to motorcycles, riding motorcycles, learning to shift, turn and brake; all within a space about the same size as a football field...and yes, it can be thrilling. But the thrill isn't just for the instructor—it can be equally thrilling for the riders. Think about it! Another rider can rear-end you, you can get T-boned by a ghost bike (launched by rider, ridden by no one), you can lose control of your own bike...*and* all those other people are watching *you!*

Hadn't mentioned that had I? The technical name for this

is *performance anxiety*...or *stage fright*. I like *performance anxiety* because it sounds better and is more appropriate; in fact, it's commonly defined as "a state of nervousness or fear which prevents or adversely affects the activity being attempted." And friends, if you're taking a basic riding course with eleven other people, you can't help it; *you do not want to be the weak one!* As an instructor I've seen sooo many people climb into their own heads and beat themselves it's actually a matter of real concern for me; when you decide you can't or you aren't doing well then shaking that belief out of you can be dang near impossible.

Really, though, isn't any endeavor pretty much damned to failure if you start with the premise: "I'm probably not going to be able to do this"? This always seems to fester and ferment into: "I can't do this." What is really depressing for a coach is to watch a student get broken by the idea that they're not doing it perfect. We don't expect *perfect*. We don't want *perfect! Perfect* is pretty dang hard to come by. Heck, there's a pretty popular religion that has the founding principle that you *can't* be perfect in action, only perfect in effort.

Perfectly executing anything—motorcycle behavior or a Reuben sandwich—is rare. And expecting perfection from yourself the first time you try something is just plain nuts. Ponder the pressure you put on yourself when you start second-guessing every single action: You're starting out from a dead stop; you slip the clutch—maybe too much; you then dump the clutch—bike lurches! You did that *wrong!* It wasn't *perfect!* People are watching! Whoaa, too much throttle, cut it, bike lurches forward; *you did it wrong!* That other rider, he's doing it great, why can't I?

That voice. The voice of pride, or fear, or whatever it is—is a confidence killer. You can *see* a rider just beat themselves down, and that cascade, once started, is almost impossible to stop. I've felt that voice before—you have, too—but it's hard to remember how hopeless it can make you feel. For me, I remember the first girlfriend; you know the first *serious* girlfriend. The first few dates and weeks you're trying soooo hard to do it right. Remember? Hold the hand. Don't hold the hand. Did; but she pulled away, was that to rub her nose *or* does she find me overbearing or needy? I'm being honest here, who knows what a fifteen or sixteen year-old boyfriend is supposed to do? All her pals have an idea what you should be doing and saying:

"Did you remember your first anniversary?" asks her best friend."

"Huh?" says you.

"It's been four weeks! This is your one month anniversary," says her best friend disgustedly. (You ask yourself: The one month—that's the Tissue Paper Anniversary, right?)

Then you stop and start working on yourself...your young mind reels—you want to be a *good* boyfriend but, a four week anniversary? When did that become important? And what do you give someone on the one month anniversary of your first date? You realize that this is just dumb, but the danger is that "the voice" is now in your head. Maybe the other guys *are* giving one month anniversary gifts...or cards...or tattoos. It seems like a milestone, but it's really a millstone! Yeah, you're suddenly in this game of "compare yourself to everyone—real or imagined."

Worst case scenario?: Her best friend says, "Well *Jared* (last boyfriend) remembered!" Off for flowers and teddy bears you go—only to realize later—Dude? That's weird. Honestly. Now imagine having that same "Am I doing this right? What is everyone else doing? Am I an idiot? Who do I listen to? What should I do? I want to be a hero not a goat!" kind of thing going full steam in your melon while you're trying to throttle, clutch, shift, and brake.

Yeah, you're doomed.

Let me tell you a motorcycle training and life secret. Don't spend your time comparing yourself to everyone else. If you're a fifty year old woman who's never sat on a motorcycle before, do *not* get into a mental death match with a twenty-two year old college tennis player who is also trying to learn to ride. That kid is younger, has more stamina, is continually taking training and coaching, and yes—isn't that worried about looking like a dork. Outcome-wise you're going to come up short.

The *best* person to compare yourself to is *yourself.* Find your own little successes and build on them. My usual routine, when I see someone beating themselves into the ground is to quickly get them out of their own heads and point out their little victories; help them realize that they are going forward.

Having a role model is great. We need heroes and examples but there's a dark side that appears when we start measuring ourselves against others: often it's comparing apples and oranges. Here's a word of advice—*Know* if you're an apple or an orange and make appropriate comparisons. Stay out of your own head. Don't worry about what others think of you, think of yourself and make fair comparisons and judgments.

Stay out of your own head, don't bring yourself down; lift yourself up! Looking for a fair evaluation of your advancement? Compare yourself to you.

# LABELS

I work with teenagers. It's rewarding, confusing, and sometimes awkward. One of the fun things is to be running around among kids and, occasionally, you recognize yourself! There's a moment when you're watching some knucklehead be a knucklehead and you think, "Hey, that's me thirty years ago!" One of the things that make the adolescent years so awkward is teens' clumsy attempts to define themselves. They aren't sure what or who they are, and they claw and swat at ideas and things that they think will make them someone. I always find it interesting to watch them buy the clothes, or get the haircut, or show off that thing that they think will be the thing that makes them unique and special.

There's a checklist that kids run down and think: If I wear this, do that, or listen to this—I'll *be* that thing. Really. Look. For every 'tween girl who's wearing Hannah Montana lip balm there's a suburban white kid wearing an untucked "long tee" and saying "fo' shizz homey." Or, there's the kids that are *totally* unique and wearing girl pants and eyeliner—*Oh* and if you don't dye your hair black or purple then, well, how can you call yourself unique? There's Emo rules you know! Scarves are old school but don't forget to have an anime haircut!

There's a playbook out there people! There always has been. Why do you think I cut the sleeves off my Molly Hatchet T-shirts? Heck, I saw a kid last month with a pink Izod and upturned collar. Hello 1980 Preppie. Need some Topsiders to go with that? Tie a sweater on and you're done! "Biff! Biff, where's the Evian?" Teens work extraordinarily hard to have the right stuff, cell phones and music players are great examples. Just wait until your kid's in middle school and see. Fender Bender, smallest of the Crashes, absolutely *had* to have a phone with a keyboard... *had to*. Luckily, I *had* to have him turn in a report card with straight As. He studied, got the As and now has a phone with a keyboard...that I can take away if the grades drop. (evil snicker)

Somehow, having a full keyboard makes him feel more complete, loved, valued, or cool. OK, he's thirteen years old, but think about your motorcycling friends—aren't we kind of the same way? At some point don't we all just want something because it's...cool?

Myself for example, I got a new jacket for Christmas. Were my old ones worn out? Naw. Had I slipped so far behind the technological curve that I needed to get a new jacket to stay on the cutting edge of safety? No. Did I switch from an unarmored jacket to an armored one? Nope, always been armored. Did I go from low visibility to Hi-Viz? Nyet. Better weather proofing/ wind proofing/water proofing? That's a big negative, GhostRider.

I got a new jacket cause it's so danged cool! Really. I dig it. Next video we shoot you'll see it! It's like a good tattoo! Why hide it? Show it off! I just like it. Does it make me a better rider? No. Does it make me more stylish? Yeah, I think so.

One of the most important questions a rider can ask themselves is, "What am I?" How do I define myself?—It's a fair question; how do you define yourself as a rider? Is it by the style of bike you ride? Is it by the riding company you keep? Is it by your riding style? Who *are* you? Why are you riding the bike you're riding? What does motorcycling do for you or your self-image? Are you riding a bike because you love to ride or because you think it will make you something you're not?

We often tell kids that clothes don't make you cool—you make the clothes cool. What you wrap yourself in doesn't define you; that's good advice like "don't straighten the pins on your hand grenades cause they might fall out!"

Although I could make this long I'm getting right to the point. *If* you decide to start riding because you look at a rider and say, *"I want to be him!"*—you're starting in a hole. You can't be him. You can only be you. You've set an impossible standard. Good luck with that Sisyphus, here's some grease to put on that rock. That's a moving target you'll never hit. You'll never be that person. You can never have the experiences they had, you can't have the thought processes or dreams or ideas they have. They are they; you are you! The sooner you stop trying to be someone else the better off you are.

*If* you buy a specific brand or type of bike because it defines who you want to be, you're still starting in a hole. It's another painful challenge. Just how is that motorcycle gonna make you fast...or smart...or cool? Some things start from the inside; Steve McQueen on *any* bike makes it look cool. But Poindexter on an MVAugusta is still...Poindexter; Poindexter with a cool bike but still Poindexter *to the bone*. I would argue that a bike *cannot* make you cool. You have to make *yourself* cool and then whatever you ride is cool by association.

Should I have poser rant here? A "wannabe 1%er" rant? No. Why? Because every flavor of motorcycle subculture has posers. They're not unique to cruisers; there are sportbike posers and adventure touring posers and dirt bike posers and sport touring posers, chopper posers, ratbike, britbike, long distance and even *anti-bike* posers. For lots of folks, motorcycles are like Paris Hilton to a fifteen year-old—damn famous, so hot, and full of "I am whatever you want me to be," that we have a entourage of wannabes and people trying to get into the glow wherever we go.

People want to be part of the motorcycle culture. Some just want to ride, some just love machines, others love the challenge of making a plan and executing it, whether it be rebuilding an old bike from their youth or riding across the country without ever being on the superslab. Others just want the camaraderie of like-minded people who are interested in the same sorts of things.

And some just know that motorcyclists are the cooooolest people they've ever seen or met and just want some of that cool to rub off. They're careful to buy the right stuff and work hard to look the right way; they worry about doing it *just right* and there's no reason we shouldn't help them out.

Yeah, I don't mind people who are infatuated with bikes and want to pose with them—because they're people who can learn to love them. My job is to grin and bear it until they change from wannabe to rider; and trust me, no one stays a wannabe forever; it's just not possible. They either blossom into a rider or they wither and disappear. So look around you; look for that annoying guy who's trying too damn hard and give him a hand. Show him how it's done. Sometimes when you kiss a frog, you find a prince.

And honestly? Weren't we all frogs once?

# FEAR

Fear is a tough thing to talk about, mostly because it's hard to define. We live in a society that values courage but is mired in caution. It's hard to be brave when you're looking to sue someone if things go wrong—there's a dissonance there that mangles the equation. So let's get right to brass tacks and define what I mean by "capital F" Fear:

FEAR—a feeling or state of being concerned for personal safety when confronted with real or imagined threats. Fear can overwhelm reason and, if allowed to continue to panic, can drive people to irrational acts.

I'm comfortable with that—definition of fear I mean. One of the crazy things about training motorcyclists is watching their mental attitudes as they approach motorcycling for the first time. Some are full of bluster and bravado, they seem to be trying to convince everyone around them that "they ain't no sissy" and "anybody can do this..." (Sometimes I worry they're trying to convince themselves). Others are dignified, almost overly serious but amazingly focused. Some, having some knowledge, are impatient and get bored easily. Some are timid and unsure of themselves...There's probably as many mind sets as there are riders.

Riders, especially in training, need to be able to recognize Fear when they feel it. That "distressing emotion" is nature's way of saying "BE CAREFUL YOU KNUCKLEHEAD!" Fear is normal, natural, and healthy. The issue I want to address is when Fear is paralytic, when Fear takes over the equation, when Fear begins to blind us to real danger and simply demand we focus on it; Fear as the distraction.

Fear wants your attention. It wants you to look and say, "This could kill me," and then step back from whatever evil, danger, or pain presents itself. What we do then is assess the situation, take any mitigating actions that seem appropriate and then either cowboy up or walk away. Sometimes, when we cowboy up and do that dangerous thing Fear becomes jealous. Like a shrieking two year-old *it* wants our attention—regardless of what you decided to do. *"Look at me!"* Fear screams, *"Don't you get this? I'M RIGHT HERE—I WILL NOT BE IGNORED!"*

Leading us to the crux of the issue: what do you do if Fear is your constant companion when you ride? What if you can't stop thinking about what the consequences of a fall are? Or how many stupid, stupid drivers there are? Or that if you brake in a turn you'll crash?

Or....or....or....or?

When you're learning to ride, and even if you're a rider, Fear, Big F capital letter Fear, shows up once in a while. We all have that moment where something frightening happens, a car pulls out, or a kid shoots off the sidewalk on a skateboard, or something falls off that truck and we pull quietly over and shake for a few moments and then stuff the Fear back into the bottle. Everybody dodges a bullet once in a while.

But what if that Fear won't go back into its cage? What if you're a beginner and you *just can't shake the Fear?* Then what?

You're human. God and DNA both want you to do one thing: *reproduce.* You can't do that if you're dead. That's what Fear does, keeps you alive to be part of your kids' lives, your grandkids', nieces', nephews'...again, Fear is nature's way of keeping you around for the good stuff. If motorcycling's too much for you—

if your mind is preoccupied with Fear—then maybe riding isn't for you. There's no shame in that! I can swim but, Man, get me out on the water a couple of miles from shore and I'm a pretty freaked out puppy. Which is one of the reasons I'm not an ocean distance swimmer. If I can't see the shore and feel reasonably comfortable I can swim to it, Fear takes a two-by-four to my face and just sits there and screams "LOOK AT ME—YOU CAN'T SWIM THAT FAR! LOOK! YOU CAN'T GET THERE FROM HERE!"

So I don't do much boating. Ain't my thing. No shame. Just that's the way it is.

If, during your training cycle you cannot stop obsessing about injury, danger, and falling, you're not focused on riding. You're distracted. You *are* a danger to yourself. Can that fear be conquered? Probably—but maybe not. Keep your head up, eyes on a swivel; fear is a good thing, fear can keep you alert and ready for action; but Fear? That paralytic, mind swallowing, consuming Fear that eats computing cycles and clouds your mind? You may need some help with that *or* maybe riding just isn't for you.

# Paperwork

"The job isn't finished until the paperwork is done." Ever hear that? It's true.

Gather round and I'll tell you the true story of the first time a policeman came to my door asking, "Do you own such and such motorcycle?"

In 1981 I turned eighteen and bought my first bike. It was a 1978 Honda XL500S. I did the deal for cash; my parents couldn't stop me; it was my great statement of personal responsibility. Of an essence it was my "I'm gonna do this and you can't stop me" moment with my parents. Thank goodness my father's reaction was, "You have insurance, right?" followed by some fatherly guidance about what "property damage" and "public liability" were and how nice insurance is...

It was a good bike, loads of fun, easy to work on, and cheap to insure. Eventually I decided to upgrade and move up to an inline four. I got my knickers all in a twist for a Suzuki GS550E. They had just put 16 inch front wheels on and baby, could they turn— not to mention they revved to what was then thought to be an impossibly high 10,500 rpms! So, I worked a deal and bought a brand spanking new GS550; which meant I had to sell the 500.

Fortunately, being a teenaged boy meant I knew loads of other teenage boys who wanted to buy it.

We had lots of discussions and pretended to haggle and eventually I sold it to a guy who I had worked with the previous summer. I signed the pink, took the cash, revelled in my role as both new-motorcycle owner and used-motorcycle seller, and then rested on my laurels.

Six weeks later there's a knock on the door which I scamper to answer. Yes, it's always shocking to open the door and have a police officer ask if you're you. Suddenly you remember everything you thought you'd got away with. I was totally flatfooted and immediately started thinking about street signs we'd liberated for girls before they left for college. (Hey, what girl going off to college doesn't want a street sign with her name on it?)

Mouth dry I say, "That's me. What can I do for you?"

"Do you own a 1978 Honda XL500S?" He asks.

"No. Yes. Well I did. But I don't anymore. I sold it. To another guy." Ever notice how you instinctively want to qualify every answer you give a law enforcement officer? Your brain starts thinking, "How can I say something in a non-incriminating way? Should I call a lawyer? Why is he asking me this? What was the last dumb stunt I pulled on the big X?" Even though you haven't owned it for well over a month, you still carry that little bag of guilt around...suddenly you're Cool Hand Luke and your dirt is in Boss Kane's yard...

As my brain clicks, ratchets, and smokes the officer looks at my poor dumb confounded teenage face and says, "According to the DMV, you still own it."

This is the kind of moment where your brain just completely locks up. You can hear the skidding rear wheel, and you just think "ahhhhhhhhhhhhhhhhhhhhhhhhhhhhhhhh." I was totally perplexed. OK. So? I mean I had sold the bike. I signed the pink. It was done. It wasn't mine anymore. I had done everything I needed to do. Game over. End of song. Why is Ponch on my doorstep?

"But I sold it," I say. I'm a motorcycle buyer/seller guy, seller as in sold it!

"Maybe you did, but the title has never been changed. You still own it."

Since you're talking to a cop, it takes a moment for your brain to unlock, and when it does you ask really, really insightful questions like: "What's it been doing?" (Like it's become some kind of killer robot ravishing Tokyo.)

"It's been reported as an abandoned vehicle," says kindly officer.

"I didn't abandon it; I sold it!" I say. Then I remember I have a bill of sale, and I ask for a moment and go rummage in my office (closet) and in my desk (shoebox) I find a crumpled up piece of paper which I run back out and hoist up in front of the officer and say, "See! Sold!"

After looking at the paper a moment he says—"Ahhhh... OK..." and then asks me to hold on a second. Remember this is back in the day before internet or WiFi or anything really powerful in the way of computers so (don't be shocked) he goes and gets on his radio. I languish on the porch for a few moments and get bored, so I wander out by his car. (Dodge Polaris—why do I know that?) Can't hear anything, worried, kinda feeling like I'm on the wrong side of Dragnet or Adam12.

Out of the car comes the officer with a clipboard and he says: "Your friend who bought the bike lives around the corner from where it's been reported as abandoned. Sounds like he has been parking it there and walking home so his parents don't find out he bought it."

Then the weirdest darn thing ever happened. He pulls out a DMV form. I expect policemen to have guns, handcuffs, road flares, billy clubs, tear gas, engines of destruction, but *not* DMV forms! Why he was packing around DMV forms I'll never know; he just laid it on me.

"This is a Title Release." I just look at it. I could not have been more shocked if he had put a severed foot in my palm. "Fill it out. Take it to the DMV. It formally says the vehicle isn't yours any more...otherwise, if we tow it, you get the bill."

He looks at me. I look at him. I say, "OK". He says, "Have a nice day," and I'm left standing there with a trip to the DMV in my hand.

Job isn't finished until the paperwork is done.

In my little nineteen year-old brain the paperwork had been done when the cash changed hands. When I signed the pink I thought I was finishing the paperwork; which wasn't true. Sometimes it's hard to know how much paperwork there really is, or where the end of it truly lays.

Your motorcycling skill set is the same way. Some times you think, "Yeah, I've learned how to ride a motorcycle, I'm skilled," and you think the paperwork is done; until you have to make that emergency maneuver and find out you can't. Went to the DMV and got your endorsement so you're done right? NO. You've done the bare minimum. Took a basic riding course? Good start; but you're not done yet! There are books you can read, videos to watch, track days, advanced rider courses, and plain ole practice.

You wouldn't learn "hello" and "goodbye" in German and then pronounce yourself fluent in the language. You'd study and work and learn and apply what you know. You wouldn't learn piano scales and then pronounce yourself a virtuoso. Learning a skill is never over. The paperwork on your skill set is never done! The minute you think you've signed the pink and the deal is done you're in real trouble. Complacency sets in. You relax in a profound sense of well-being without understanding the risks around you.

Keep riding. Keep reading. Keep learning. Take a training course. Hone your craft. Remember: with motorcycles, the paperwork is never finished.

# ADVICE

Ever get bad advice? The "why did I listen to that guy" kind of bad advice? *Wait*—don't answer that. Let's talk about *good* advice. Has someone ever given advice and you carried it around with you and one day, suddenly, it pays off? Remember, advice isn't always that Shakespearian "to thine own self be true" stuff. Advice can be very focused and to the point. You'll get lots of motorcycle advice like: "always put your kickstand down when you fill up" or "keep your cellphone in your jacket so if you get separated from your bike it's with you." Advice is easy to come by—and you never know when it's gonna come in handy.

I work as a freelance camera operator at large, multiple camera sporting events. A couple of times a year I get to do rodeo. Rodeo is fun because I keep a few cows, a bull, and a couple of horses and it's fun to hang out with cowboys and act all "rancher." One thing I've noticed about cowboys is that they are a religious bunch. You wouldn't believe how many of them are back there behind the chutes praying right before they get on rough stock (bareback/saddle bronc/bull riding). I know because I usually stand on the back side of the chutes with them and get those shots where they strap in and then the gate flings open and all hell breaks loose.

Bullfighters intrigue me also. They'll get right in there with those big ole bulls and smack them around and distract them so cowboys can get away. Its nuts—until you talk to them and you find out they are truly professionals. They know what they're doing, it's not just a dive in there and hope the bull doesn't kill you enterprise, they have a craft and they hone their craft.

I was talking to a bullfighter once and I asked, "How do you keep from getting squished like a bug?" He replied, "*If* a bull comes after you, run like hell; then, right when you're sure you're gonna die, take one more step and turn right or left as hard as you possibly can." Turns out bulls can't turn on a dime. Watch sometime. Bullfighters turn *inside* the turning radius of a bull, they wait till the bull's right there and then they turn tighter than the bull. The bull goes wide, often loses interest, and game over.

Tricky part is you can't turn too early or the bull can adjust his line and still get you; hence the "run till you're sure you're gonna die and *take one more step*." That little bit of advice is designed to make sure you don't turn too early. Neat advice but when are you gonna use it? Probably never—unless you own a bull like I do. My bull (2000 lbs.) got out the other day. He jumped the fence to romance the ladies in the next pasture. Part of bull romance means beating up the bull those ladies belonged to. By the time I got there he had been three rounds and was doing OK. We got him separated and PFC Crash and I were trying to get him into the neighbor's corral to load him into the trailer when things went a little sideways. What made me think that bull would find me soooo intimidating I'll never know; I just went up to an animal that had been beating up another one ton animal and figured—"yeah, he'll do what I tell him".

Let me just say this: when an animal that weighs ten times what you do and looks *down* on you starts running at you—that's a breathtakingly frightening moment. As I started running for my life, suddenly these words of advice came to my mind: "*If* a bull comes after you, run like hell; then, right when you're sure you're gonna die, *take one more step* and turn right or left as hard as you possibly can".

Running like hell was easy. I looked over my shoulder, and the bull was right there, head down; I could feel him back there breathing. I thought "I think I might die," took a couple more steps, then when I was *sure* I was gonna die, I *TOOK ONE MORE STEP*, and turned left as hard as I could. I looked back over my left shoulder to see what was happening and the bull veered off to the right and ran a few more yards before stopping and giving me the evil eye.

I turned to the wide-eyed PFC Crash (who was astonished his old man was first, alive and second, could still move pretty dang fast) and I said, "I believe we'll just leave him alone a while."

What does any of this have to do with motorcycles you ask? A lot! Because advice on motorcycling, solicited and unsolicited, is shockingly easy to get once you're "outed" as a motorcyclist. Once you're tagged as a rider, advice starts flowing in. Your family may give you motorcycle advice in the forms of "riding is crazy!" or "sell it" or just "Be Safe!" Your biking friends have loads of advice; some good, some bad. TV has advice about motorcycles, ever see a public service announcement to "Look Twice for Bikes"? I've found that advice about bikes is easy to get; just as advice about bullfighting is easy to get. You can get it in the stands at the rodeo—go up to the beer line and start talking bullfighting and someone's gonna tell you how it's done. You *might* get good advice or you *might* get crap advice. If you want to know about bullfighting maybe the best place to find out about it is from bullfighters; *real* PCRA bullfighters, not the 44oz kind in the beer line.

Motorcycles are the same way. Look for good source material; you can read things like *Proficient Motorcycling* by David Hough, or *Ride Hard, Ride Smart* by Pat Hahn. Sportbikers will like *Sport Riding Techniques* by Nick Ienatsch. Or you can take an MSF course or find a local track school. Online offers great possibilities too, like http://www.msgroup.org/ which has everything from a "vault speed calculator" (how fast were you traveling when you got launched—you mad projectile you) to forums on how to get started riding. Another great beginners site is http://www.beginnerbikers.org/ or http://www. motorcycleforum.com/ I like them all. Are they the only forums out there? *No!* I also like http://www.motorcycle-journal.com/ and http://www.squidbusters.com/ Odds are you can find like-minded people and get good, sound advice somewhere out there online. Just Google "motorcycle" and you'll be shocked at the amount of help out there.

Do you get nutty advice sometimes? Sure, just be ready to ignore some. Just because I don't take bullfighting advice from guys in the beer line doesn't mean you won't meet a bullfighter in the beer line.

These are sites and references I'm comfortable with. Hough-Hahn-Ienatsch?—I trust them. MSF?—Trustworthy. Websites?—Well, I wouldn't mention them if I didn't trust them but the bottom line is you have to decide who *you* trust. Remember that motorcycle saying "It's just me and my bike baby"? It is. *You* have to decide who you trust. I will tell you one thing: when that moment comes and you realize you're in trouble, it's pretty darn comforting to know someone who knows what they're doing has given you a bit of advice to hang your hopes on.

"Increase pressure on the inside hand grip—the bike will lean more" has gotten me out of trouble just like, "run like hell; then, right when you're sure you're gonna die, take one more step and turn right or left as hard as you possibly can" did. Don't be afraid to talk about bikes and how to ride—you never know when you're gonna need a nugget to get you out of trouble.

Oh! How did we finally get that bull taken care of? We used another piece of advice Grandpa Crash gave me: "Use the right tool for the job." We went and got the horse.

# ART & SCIENCE

Ever notice how failed artists end up as critics? You know, they understand the science of something but simply can't apply the art? Ever had an "artless" doctor? You know, the one with "no bedside manner." He's the guy who can tell you what's wrong and what has to be done but does it so ineptly that you want to run away. Rather than, "We'll need to get inside to really fix it," they say, "We'll start with a McBurney incision diagonally down the abdominal wall, using electrocautery to control bleeding..." at which point you run screaming from the room.

I've known a few artless teachers—people that just love their area of expertise but just can't relate to students. There's a saying that "elementary teachers teach because they love kids, secondary teachers teach because they love their subject." Ever have a math or chemistry teacher who loved their subject but didn't particularly like kids? Me too. Arrggggggggggggh.

Think of the clumsy carpenter, the guy who can use all the tools, knows which tool does what and why and how...and then can't frame a square wall for love or money. You see it in recreational painters, who know how to put the paint on the canvas but can't make it speak. Adhering to all the rules and conventions they think they're making art, but all they are doing is soullessly following a map. Correct brush, good canvas, right paints, rules of composition, complimentary colors, proper lighting, holding the brush right, good palette control, shading as instructed...crap painting. No soul. No center. No life. No art.

Don't get me wrong; I'm not talking about a lack of interest or desire! Something else is missing, something wonderful and wild and intangible just isn't there. They can still love something but they're lacking the ability to apply it with passion and faith and abandon. Part of the pain of watching someone who dearly loves something but has no craft—no art—is that they often apply the science and then become confused that the art isn't there. They *did everything right*, but it's not art. Sometimes they don't know it! They think the art is in possessing the science. They figure if they master the science that art will naturally follow. It's a calculation they hope to use. Art, however, is fluid and if there was a simple formula to apply we'd all be Dutch Masters.

But the art of it is taking the science and getting something out of it that isn't in the calculations. Breathing life into the science makes a great teacher. Making the colors come alive is more than just using complimentary ones. A great table has more than good joints and matching grain; the wood flows and the joints melt and the table becomes more than just planks glued together, it becomes a new thing: *Art*.

Ever watch those football stars on the dancing show? They were artists on the football field. Some can dance as well! Others go through the motions and it's all there but it's not right. The right foot is in the right place but things just...aren't...*art*.

Motorcycles are an excellent example of this problem. I really, truly believe that the great riders you see are blessed with a childlike faith in the art of motorcycling—they may be aware of the science but it's the art they trust. They ride well, not because of calculation, but because of aptitude. Aptitude just means they possess a gift of listening to the bike, a sense of feedback that allows them to hear what the bike tells them and get the most out of the thing. They aren't burdened by the calculation of riding, they embrace the craft of riding.

Example: Counter steering. You can spend your entire life learning about deflection and camber thrust and rolling resistance and the coefficient of friction, but knowing all those things doesn't mean you can apply them, just like knowing scales or how a piano physically works doesn't make you a concert pianist. It's when science meets aptitude that beautiful things start to happen. Be aware, aptitude alone isn't enough, just as science isn't.

I can muddle around on the guitar. I can play weird things like Christmas carols and hymns, Greensleeves and Godzilla... frankly, it's enough to be interesting at parties and I can calm myself when I'm tense. I'm extraordinarily average with a classical guitar. I know how it works. I practice once in a while but there's no way that I'm gonna be the next Segovia that ain't happenin' *ever*. I could practice my brains out 24/7 and still only become more technically astute. I don't play with a lot of soul. I just can't make a guitar "gently weep."

Some are blessed with "it" or the "x-factor." Some people just can do it; they just are naturally gifted at something. Others can't do it and never will; and still the largest body of all simply can only "get it done." The danger is when we think that technical understanding can replace that "x-factor"; that if we just do it enough we'll be more than proficient—we'll be Masters, that somehow from rough knowledge we'll pull finished art.

I believe that sometimes we meet Masters who delve deeply into science. Guys like Keith Code and David Hough who, as they master the art, master the science. I also believe that this may be a one way street—you can master the art and *then* master the science, but trying to master the science and *then* the art, well, I'm not sure that works.

I've seen people become hung up on "is my arm in the right position?" or "as a percentage—how much weight should I put on the front while doing U-turns?" and "in hours, how much practice should I do before I get on the freeway?"

My answers are simple: "Were you comfortable and could control the bike? Then your arm is in the right position." "Did you make the U-turn? Then you had it right." and "How many hours 'til you get on the freeway? You'll know when you're ready. Listen to the little voice."

There is no *perfect* way to ride a motorcycle, it's not like mixing fertilizer—it's more like cooking! Part science, part art. The moment you become locked into your recipe and can't adjust it to taste is the moment you go from artist to chemist. Likewise, the moment you take that living, quivering, slobbering calculation that is a motorcycle and demand it act the same exact way every single time in every single situation is the moment you've killed the art of riding. Why? Because the variables of riding are what trumps the science. Every situation isn't the same and the great ones, the artists, they adjust at a core, visceral level—they ride with their gut.

Artless riding isn't worth doing. The moment a timid or unsteady rider wants to discuss the physics of riding, get ready to run 'cause that rider doesn't want to ride a bike, they want to control it and break it and make it do their will. Me? I'd rather ride. My advice: Learn the physics of riding, but good heavens, don't smother your spirit with science; and if the idea that a mechanical animal has a soul, unique properties, and a mind of its own offends you, then we're probably not gonna get along...

# LIES ADULTS TELL

Think back, through the eons of time, yes way back to when you were a teenager. If you're a guy you had hair on your head not in your ears, and if you're a gal, well…let's not say 'cause I don't want to offend half the planet.

Remember the lies adults told you? You know, the ones that were intended to keep you safe from harm and danger. Earnest, hopeful lies! Lies like: "Everyone who smokes dies of cancer." Wait. They don't. How about this one?: "Nothing good ever happens after midnight." Pardon? Most of the real fun I had started after midnight. Granted, bad things happened as well.

OH, OH, OH! Ever hear this one? "They *think* they're having fun, but they're not!" You knew that one was a lie from the word go. *Nobody* gets on that train.

These were all lies that were intended to make us safer and happier.

"Eat your spinach; it'll make you strong like Popeye." *Not.*

"You will lose an eye if you get a BB gun." Got the gun—still have both eyes. My kids all have BB guns and all their eyes.

"Never be alone with a girl!" Yeah, see, slow dancing kinda started me thinking this might be a lie. Further research proved my initial hypothesis (girl + Crash + alone = GOOD) was correct. Since having children myself I have since revised my risk/reward calculation and encourage my kids *not* be alone with the opposite sex unless in public...at a restaurant...in the afternoon... with me nearby with a taser.

"If you speed you'll have an accident"—had one; wasn't speeding; got a "no fault due to weather" from the CHP.

"If you stick your arm out the window it'll get torn off!" Still flapping and driving.

Our parents, teachers, mentors, doctors, zookeepers, and uncles all told us well-intended lies. They tried to get us to change our unsafe behaviors by painting the worst possible outcome and then saying: IT WILL HAPPEN—and then it doesn't and our parents, teachers, mentors, doctors, zookeepers, and uncles are all proven liars—well-intentioned liars, but liars none-the-less. As teens we realize these "well intended lies" for what they are, which can be very upsetting because no matter how well intended—they were lies. People had been actively giving us inaccurate, yet benevolently wrong information.

Not everyone who ran away from home wound up a teenage prostitute. You *could* cut class and still pass. Loud music didn't leave you deaf. (But, Ted Nugent if you're reading this, I'd like the top 10K cycles back.) The government *did* lie. About the only thing I can think of that we all got told that is really, absolutely, 100% true was:

"Money doesn't grow on trees." I use that one now myself.

When my brother's friends started showing up with motorcycles one of the things that people started telling me was: "Everyone who rides one of those gets killed." Time went by, and I patiently waited for them to die. Yet they didn't. They didn't even crash. Day after day I'd see them around, and they managed to cheat death. Time went by, another motorcycle showed up (Yamaha RD400 Daytona), and prophets of doom predicted death for all. The ferryman never came. A Yamaha XS750 appeared in another friend's hands—surely death was gonna catch one of these guys! But *no!* Not even a serious crash.

These well-intended lies are unfortunately prevalent in the motorcycling community still today. We tell these well-intended lies because they encourage smart behavior; we lie to try and help people make wise choices. Yet, just like teens, riders fundamentally sniff out these well-intended lies.

Here's a few:

4. "If you don't go ATGATT (All The Gear All The Time) you'll be sorry."

No you won't. You *might* be sorry someday but there's a distinct possibility that you may never hit the pavement and will never need the gear. See, we want people to wear the gear. We want them to be ready *if* something goes bad and it's easier to overstate the case than take the time to explain that gear is a personal choice and will make you more comfortable and protect you from injury. However, we don't want to admit that you might never need it. Go to Sturgis or Daytona—you'll find thousands and thousands of people who never wore gear—and they aren't sorry. The danger is in needing gear and not having it. The consequences are staggering. Risk is a terribly personal issue. I won't risk riding without gear. Others will. I suggest you wear the gear. Does that mean you'll be sorry if you don't? Maybe. Maybe not. Honestly? It's not worth the risk to ride without it.

3. "It's not *if* you crash, it's *when* you crash."

Lie. Not everyone crashes. Some fall, some fall at speed, but not every single one. This is the bastard cousin of "everyone who rides—dies." The difference is that it's designed to make riders who fall feel better about themselves. It's a selfish lie but it's also intended as a warning—gravity works, be careful but don't resign yourself to a crash.

2. "My bike won't do that."

WTF? Ask someone to ride a U-turn in twenty-five feet and they will actually tell you, "My bike won't do that." Meaning "I can't do a tight U-turn." This is a stepsister to "Bikes are all totally different, dirtbikes have nothing in common with cruisers and cruisers have nothing in common with sportbikes which have nothing in common with adventure tourers..." Lies all. The basic physics of motorcycles are the same, some react quicker, turn tighter, brake or accelerate faster, but this is akin to saying the only *real* dogs are German Shepherds. *A dog is a dog.* If you can't make your dog behave or don't think you can—just say it! "Sorry that's too tight for me" would work. The minute you start saying things like "my bike won't" someone like Motorman Mike will prove it will, and you'll feel silly. Yeah, it's OK to say "I'm not comfortable doing that." Why don't I ride to Daytona for the races? I'm not comfortable being on the road that long. There, truth.

1. "If you don't wear a helmet you'll end up a vegetable."

Nope. First it assumes the "everyone crashes" lie and second, it assumes that all motorcycle accidents result in you smacking your melon against something. This is probably the most tempting lie to tell, so tempting in fact, that I have found it on my lips. However, not every bike crashes, not every rider falls and not every head hits the pavement. I recently read about a rider with over 500,000 miles of accident free riding—and yes, he rode with a helmet! Now here's the weird part—his helmet has never saved him from injury due to falling—therefore, did he need it? His accident free career may be the most persuasive argument you can make for *not* wearing a helmet!

*Don't take this to mean I endorse not wearing helmets—Wear your freakin' lid!!!*

The consequences of smacking your unprotected head on the pavement are dire and frightening. Always wear a helmet. Why? It's a risk/reward calculation. The risks of smacking your head on the pavement outweigh the rewards of not wearing a helmet. *Wear your lid.* Helmets also protect you from weather, animal and insect impact, wind, noise and crap kicked up from the road. *You should always wear a helmet.*

Do you know why cops carry guns? The same reason you should wear a lid—not because you *will* need it, but you *might* need it!

I'm not gonna lie to you. Lying to you assumes you're not very bright and weakens my case. One look around and you'll see that not everybody dies from riding without the proper gear *or* having proper training. The consequences of riding unprotected can be expensive, painful, and permanent and so I will say this: wear the gear; not wearing it isn't worth the risk.

Don't try to scare people into wise behaviors by telling benevolent lies; change their minds with the truth. Ask the real questions like: what if you're not wearing a helmet and you fall? Can you live with the consequences of striking your head to the pavement at twenty mph? My wife can't. My kids can't. My friends can't. I can't. A nice haircut won't do you any good when what you really need is a good helmet.

There is no power in telling well-intended lies; instead tell your helmetless friends the truth: you love them the way they are and if things all go to hell, a helmet will help keep them that way.

# Poo

Here's an axiom we use in my room at school: "If you start with poo, there's not much you can do." Poo is, by definition, poo—what can you do to make it better? You can dress it up, you can paint it, mold it, make it look like a rose; but it's still *poo*. It's an important idea for kids who are trying to learn video production to grasp. They hear that old saying "we'll fix it in post" and think it's an excuse for poor production values. Didn't level your tripod? Picture runs downhill right? Off kilter? Yes, you *can* fix it in post—by compromising the image. Scale it up, rotate it, get it straight and level, *but* upscaling the image will stretch it and potentially you lose image quality *and* your composition changes as you zoom in on the image; it's no longer the image you originally wanted. The picture is level but you lost some quality doing it.

The same applies with color issues. You can manipulate the image to try and *make* it look right but it's important to remember: your trying to make it *look* right, not *make* it right. Making it right means the original quality of the image is right. Once you have a poorly crafted shot, unless your name is Peabody and you have a Way Back Machine, all you're doing

is, in the parlance of my military friends, "polishing the turd."
Ouch.

Harsh but true. Some things you can't fix. Got an out of focus
shot? There's no "Focus" filter in Photoshop or AfterEffects that
will take an out of focus image and make it focused. Underexpose
something? Once you've captured the image you can't find
information that isn't there, you can change the levels and get
the stuff you can see to look brighter but if it's in the shadows
and underexposed, its gone. Under or over exposed information
is gone like Jimmy Hoffa on a Wednesday afternoon in 1975. It's
just gone and never to be seen again.

Learning video production students need to realize that
pre-production and production are important, make that vital,
parts of creating a good video. Crap pre-production leads to
crap production which terminates in post production hell as
you look backward in time and try to fix mistakes that, in most
cases, can't be fixed—only mediated. Tattoo removal comes
to mind here. Often instead of removing a tat you'll see them
covered up. It's my understanding that "fixing" tattoos is a
vibrant part of the industry of ink. (Wrong name on your bum?
We can cover that up!) Advice? Take care in choosing your
tattoos; and avoid inking names on yourself. "Mom" might not
even be safe—what if she cuts you out of the will?

Video, like tattooing, rewards a good plan and can punish
you for a bad one; motorcycling is the same way. Killing a bad
idea in its infancy is easier than killing it when it's in flower. It's
like a weed, you can pluck out a small one but wait too long and
you've nurtured something that's got thorns and thistle and then
it's time to get the shovel and gloves 'cause like, well, this is gonna
take some time and work to fix.

*No one* gets up in the morning and says, "Today I'll wreck my
life; today I shall damage myself beyond repair, end my career
or tank my marriage." Those sorts of disasters start somewhere,
usually as a small oversight or poor judgment that just starts
to grow. When things go wrong in our lives we need to be the
National Transportation Safety Board; we need to go looking

for that "root cause"; the place where the chain of events started.

Often, it's due to a lack of planning or as we call it in videoworld, *pre*-production. Bad pre-production leads to bad production; bad production is like a crappy boyfriend or girlfriend—once you've got one you're reluctant to let them go 'cause finding another is a real pain. We hang on to the things we know, and we don't want to abandon something we've plowed time and energy into.

Motorcycle example: Planning is important. A vital part of my planning for a motorcycle ride is fuel management. My current and all time favorite motorcycle has a teeny tiny gas tank—2.6 gallons. That's not much. In stock trim my bike will get about 70 miles per gallon (your mileage may vary). *Mine*, with modifications, gets about 55mpg. Why does this matter? Who cares? *I do!* Because I need to find a gas station *every* 125 miles...or start to push, or hitchhike...does anyone hitchhike anymore? See where I'm going here? Who stops for strangers on the side of the road? I digress.

I use the age old motorcycle fuel management technique—I reset my trip odometer every time I fill up. I then have to keep an eye on my odometer. I know at 102 miles I'm going to get that sputtering that tells me to flip the fuel switch to reserve because I've got 30 or so miles left before I'm walking a motorcycle instead of riding it.

The tricky part is not letting things get away from you. Say I'm going for a ride on a Saturday morning, and I fill up the night before. In the morning, as I leave the odometer starts running. Now, this is where things start to feel like a nasty seventh grade "story problem" but if you have a small gas tank, won't do the math, and don't have a plan—you end up walking. After I leave my house and when I reach the bottom of the canyon I've gone 32 miles. Luckily, there's a gas station in Boise at the bottom of the hill—so I can refill my tank and reset my odometer. Then it's up the hill. The next gas station is 34 miles up the road in Idaho City; *meaning* if I don't stop there and fuel up I have 90 or so miles to empty. Here's the tricky part—once I leave that gas station I have only one course of action, I *have* to go to Lowman (where there is no gas) and then turn left and go to Garden Valley; it's the only gas I can reach and it's 68 miles away. *If* I want to turn right and go to Stanley I *have* to fuel up in Idaho City; fueling up at the bottom of the hill I can only reach Garden Valley. Why? Because Stanley is 94 miles from Idaho City. That's 126 miles from the gas station in Boise.

Basically, once I'm in Idaho City I have to commit to a plan; it's a waypoint where I *have* to make a decision. Why? Because not getting gas means going to Garden Valley...*but* getting gas means I can either go to Stanley *or* go to Garden Valley. See the difference? Getting fuel gives me options; not topping off makes a decision.

In fact, not getting gas could lead to disaster! What if I don't get gas and when I get to Garden Valley the gas station is closed? Then the next fuel stop in Horseshoe Bend, another 21 miles down the road from Garden Valley *or* 116 miles from the bottom of the hill. That's right on the edge of fuel range.

Boy. That's a lot of math *and* a fair amount of thinking. It turns out that lots of folks don't like to do either, calculate or think. Let's think simple: remember that old cliché "A journey of a thousand miles starts with one step"? Here's my advice—*step in the direction you want to go!* Having a good idea where the next step is going to land is a good idea as well.

Where's the poo in all this? Simple, do you have what it takes to admit you stepped the wrong way? In your soul is there the bald faced honesty to admit that you have a bad plan, crap directions, and poor execution? Can you look, suck it up and forthrightly state: *"I stepped in poo"*? I've found that once I've got my teeth into an idea I often lose perspective, get too focused and then can't let a bad idea go; the urge to take a crap idea and somehow pound it into art is hard to resist. Ever see someone who's addicted to something? That just has to have it? Can't leave it alone? You can drag them away from it and you know that they're thinking about it—mulling it, chewing it, trying to find a way to get back to it.

Bad ideas are that way—you'll dump more energy into trying to somehow contort it into something good than you'd ever spend if you simply stopped, backed up, and started again. Being married to a bad idea is a spiritual money pit; no matter what or how much you pour in, you'll never get ahead of it.

Polishing the turd, that's what that is.

True story: One time I left Idaho City without topping off the gas tank; that's not unusual, it just means I've thrown all in and am going to Garden Valley. On my ride I got to Lowman where I should have turned left but instead, I went straight up the road to Stanley; a destination I *knew* I probably couldn't reach...unless, maybe if I was easy on the throttle I could squeak out a couple of MPG...*or* I could coast on the downhill stuff...*or,* well, my gas calculations are always overly conservative. There I was, the odometer rolling up miles, riding along the river, in a beautiful gorge, looking at ponderosa pine, and looking for elk in the meadows *and* trying to convince myself, "Yeah, I can do this! Keeping the revs downs, I can do this."

Yeah, and maybe if I hope enough I'll suddenly get 2 inches taller! And some of that hair that started disappearing at thirty will grow back! *And* I can pay the deficit down with my mind!

In my pea-sized brain I was working on my "point of know return," the mileage point that I *know* I can get to Garden Valley. But I couldn't let my bad idea go. I stopped at the edge of my original calculations to think. I realized I had to turn around and head to Garden Valley; but boy, I *did not* want to. I had this really bad idea, I had pushed it right to the edge, and now; like a guy with a crappy girlfriend; I had bought a diamond, had it in my pocket and was about to *fully commit* to a strikingly bad course of action. I had flirted with it, dated it, loved it up, fought, realized it was bad, stuck with it anyway, and now it was show time. Was I all in? I was like Nixon, sitting in the White House after the break in—do I hang G. Gordon and Co. out to dry? Do I stick with it? Cover up? Confess? Start firing Attorneys General? Call in the CIA for some convenient "heart attacks" or call Walter Cronkite and explain?

On the way back to Garden Valley, I hit reserve on the tank a lot earlier than I would have liked and at the gas station I put 2.2 gallons in the tank but, I made it—just barely.

I took a bad idea and almost chased it to minor, annoying disaster. Why? Because a crap plan is a crap plan and sometimes you let them die, other times you have to kill them. Either way one thing we all need to do is learn to let it go. Why? Because poo is poo and always will be.

# WAKING UP *NOT* DEAD...YET!

I believe it was F. Scott Fitzgerald who said, "In the real dark night of the soul, it's always three o'clock in the morning..." I'm not sure I agree, but I can tell you this: at three o'clock in the morning it's really, really dark. Unless there's a full moon and no clouds—but I'm waffling.

I have diabetes and sometimes, in the dark soul of the night (3am) I'll wake up with a low blood glucose level. Annoying though it is I'm happy to wake up; the alternative isn't too appealing. When I was twenty-seven the warranty on my pancreas apparently expired and it quit working which means I produce no insulin. 100 years ago I'd have died before my second child's second birthday. 50 years ago odds are I'd have eyesight issues, heart disease, kidney problems, and have died early and (potentially) ugly.

Nowadays, I suffer from no real adverse effects. My feet haven't started to die underneath me. My heart is in great shape. If you don't catch me taking my glucose level or shooting insulin you'd never know I'm a Type I diabetic.

One of the only adverse effects I do suffer from is one I bring on myself: I over shoot insulin and wake up in the night with a low blood glucose level. Quick Biology lesson time! Insulin facilitates getting sugars from your bloodstream into your cells. Too little insulin means sugars back up in your bloodstream, your body tries to flush them out through your kidneys, hence tremendous thirst and plenty of peeing. Too much insulin and you'll shovel all the sugar out of your bloodstream and then bad things like comas can set in. Remember Claus Von Bulow? He was accused of killing his wife with an insulin induced coma.

Insulin, especially since it's usually self administered, can be as dangerous as it is lifesaving! When your sugars crash, you get the shakes, sweats, and lose short term memory and higher brain function. Basically you can end up acting like you're on a three day bender. I once had a conversation with a policeman who had chased a car down a major street; the car had struck thirteen other vehicles before it struck a (get this, karma fans) a parked flatbed tow truck. The guy in the car couldn't stand up.

He had low blood glucose caused by insulin. It's surprisingly easy to screw up your insulin calculations. Too high a blood sugar equals a high A1C number, which warns of all the associated diabetic complications—heart disease, kidney issues, neuropathy, sight issues, and circulation problems in your feet. When you're trying to get tight control of your sugars you'll sometimes make mistakes. The tricky part is recognizing when things are going sour. (That's a diabetic joke—get it? Low blood sugar = sour? High blood sugar = sweet? Diabetes! A laugh a minute happy good time!)

My personal experience with low glucose levels is that my symptoms have changed over time. When I was first diagnosed I would get the sweats and shakes when I was low. I could hold my hand out in front of me and watch it quiver. Beads of sweat would pop out in my hairline. Symptoms were clear and obvious. Over the course of time my symptoms have changed. Now days I don't get the shakes or sweats anymore; I get sick to my gut *and* I get goofy or mean. Mrs. Crash never saw me back in the day when I was a surly kid and used to drink a little (sorry Mom). Currently, when I have a low glucose it's as close to being drunk as I ever get now. I forget what you just said to me. I'm confused. I'm goofy. Sometimes I'm meaner than nails, I'll bare my teeth and snap at you. It just varies. Best thing is that I can recognize immediately that something is wrong. Even in my compromised state I can get my brain to say, "something isn't right," and then check to see what it is.

Here's the coolest part of all. If I have a low glucose level in the middle of the night, I'll wake up. Just snap right awake and know "I'm low." If you were to visit the Crash hacienda you'll find in the kitchen, every night, a blood glucose monitor sitting out and open on the counter ready for use. Why? Because when I wake up at three o'clock in the morning odds are my sugars have crashed. Waking up not dead is a good thing. The Lord looks out for fools and small children—you decide which I am.

I like waking up not dead...or in a coma. I'm lucky. Others aren't. Want to have some fun? Google "hypoglycemia deaths" and look at all the "hypoglycemia preceding fatal car collisions" and "Dead in Bed Syndrome"; it can be rather sobering to look at how a simple screw up on your math can lead you to disaster. Not to say that being a Type 1 diabetic means you're gonna accidently kill yourself, by all means there's plenty of other things that can just as easily get you—from drunk drivers to flesh eating bacteria to falling down in the shower.

Everyone who injects insulin will eventually miscalculate; they will experience hypoglycemia, low blood sugars. As a rule: they won't wake up "Dead in Bed." It's just one of the possible negative outcomes. Wonderful thing for me? When I'm low— I wake up!

Knowing something isn't right and then *acting* on it can be a tough issue for diabetics. I wake up in the night, I'm tired, the house ain't warm, it's 2:23 in the morning—and I don't want to get up. I hate the way my toes feel when they're cold, that "skin's too tight" feeling you get when your toenails are starting to chill. Back in the day, when the kids were younger I'd always step on a Lego in the dark and that hurts! Getting out of bed is a pain. Staying in bed however, really doesn't solve any problems; it can make them worse. If I wake up feeling wrong I get up and do something about it. Just like when I'm riding and things don't feel right.

You've had that haven't you? That flickering light in the back of your mind that says, "something's wrong"? Like when, in the blur of the morning routine, you grab the toothbrush and start scrubbing away and the voice is saying "something's not right" and you shift your weight from foot to foot, you pull up your PJs, or look to see if a light bulb is burned out; then looking in the mirror you realize that there's a blue toothbrush sticking out of your mouth when *your* toothbrush is red. Yikes. (You never admit that to your kid do you? That one goes to the grave.)

That instinct, that ability to say: something isn't right, wake up and look around; that's a blessing. Where it comes from I do not know. It could be that we're creatures of habit and pattern so when things are a little askew the back of our brain starts getting jumpy and reaches out to shake our consciousness.

It could be precognition of some kind. Maybe as our brains sort out that things aren't as they should be, the alarms are going off and that feeling is the precursor to awareness of something we innately know but are not conscious of yet.

Our challenge, our gift or our curse is our ability to *hear* and *act* on those murmurings our subconscious brain sends out. As a diabetic the sooner I sense something wrong the better off I'm going to be. It's the same with riding; it's the same with life.

# BACKGROUND MUSIC

I was standing out in front of the high school the other day as parents picked up their students. It was an early release day; finals were being administered and they went home after a half day. Oh, come on, their brains are all melted after an AP Trig test; give them a break. To point, I was out front and the cars were pulling up and the soccer moms and dads were picking up their "too cool for soccer" kids and I suddenly realized that as each child opened the door I could clearly *hear* what their mothers and fathers were listening too.

I first noticed this because a student ran up to a car, opened the door, and an indignant male voice came blasting out. My "teacher-sense" tingled and I was literally rolling forward on the balls of my feet to walk up and ask, "Is everything OK?" when I realized I recognized the voice! It was Rush Limbaugh— and boy, was he pissed. Someone had "dragged his name into" something. Don't know what. Door closed, car pulled off, the smell of acerbic anger wafted in the air, hung there a moment, and dissipated. Gone. So I started thinking: how's that for the background music for the "how did your test go sweetie" conversation? Think about it a minute. You get into the car with your mom and a pissed-off Rush and maybe you didn't do so well on that AP History exam—or that geometry final. Yeah, that's a hostile work environment. (Of course if the conversation is about the evils of the "Socialist Education System," a smart kid has a good shot at deflecting the blame... Dang teachers!)

True story: When I worked at the Fox affiliate in the Boise market I was a Commercial Producer/Director. Sounds big and important but really I just made spots for the station's clients. Could be a car dealer, could be a pawn shop, could be family restaurant; I just made all kinds of commercials. I was in the production department and we had three producers and one production manager. Every couple of days we producers would get together in the morning and decide what song we would "song plant" on the boss. Figuring out a song we could all hum or whistle might take a moment but when the boss arrived we'd all make sure to whistle or hum it around him. *If you decide to song plant someone make sure you get a song they know.* Insipid, annoying pop songs work great—here, I'll song plant you right now: *Don't hum the hook from "Macarena."* There. When you're sitting at dinner tonight eating meatloaf, try not to hum that.

A good song plant is like a garlic burp. It's in there, it travels with you, and pops up when you least expect it *and* you'll never know when it will sneak out—it just does. (If you're in the bathroom whistling "Macarena" later, don't blame me.)

What is the background music in your life? What runs through your head as you get out of the car or step off the bike or just have a quiet moment at work? We've all got some kind of song plant in our heads. (I heard the theme song from "Happy Days" the other day and found myself humming it as I watched my Broadcasting 02 students taking their semester final.)

Confessional: I sing when I ride. I sing to myself. Could be anything—it might even be nonsense I'm making up on the fly. But it's something I do. Does it mean I'm bored?

Maybe, maybe not. But it's the song plants from the last few hours that will bubble up to the surface. Listen right now and you'll hear the same in my voice as I say this; often I'll find myself singing jingles, or TV theme songs. (I can, and do sing the theme song from "Super Chicken." Google it. *Best thing ever!*)

Kids at our school aren't allowed to use iPods during school hours. The way I catch them is by listening. When they listen they'll turn it up so loud I can hear it. Here's a music axiom: angry kids listen to angry music. Another obvious secret: depressed kids listen to depressing music. Here's some evident truth: kids trying to get amped up for a football game like to listen to loud, exciting, angry, up music.

I'm not saying music is bad or talk radio is bad I'm asking you this: what is the background music of your life? What's on your playlist? What do you ruminate over? (Ruminate means to turn things over in your mind...like a cow chewing it's cud...and it means chewing cud too.) Yeah, standing in line at the DMV what happens in your mind? What do you hear inside your head? Not just in the quiet times but when the winds in your helmet and the revs are just right *or* what do you hear when traffic's stopped and no one's going anywhere and you don't dare lane split because it's considered "reckless driving" in the state you live in? What do you hear? What's the muzak playing in the elevator of your head?

May I offer an idea? Why do angry kids listen to angry music? Do they listen to spend their anger? To express it somehow and let it go? Or do they listen to build it? And once all that anger is inside you—how do you get rid of it? Is it there forever? Does it fade? I used to listen to a fair amount of angry music, and it pops up here and there when I'm on the bike and running hard with someone, being a little too aggressive, getting up on the tank and...getting angry. It's a good sign from my subconscious that things are going to a dark and dangerous place.

That's when I sing the "Super Chicken" theme song.

Maybe it's time to think about the mood we put ourselves in. The things we carry into the day with us. Do the things you surround you with make you a better person or a bitter person? Do you see light ahead or darkness? Are you singing "Super Chicken" or "Mr. Crowley" in your mind?

Is it helping or hurting?

Monday, Tuesday, Happy Days...Wednesday, Thursday, Happy....DANG IT!

# BLAME

Here's the dealio: I teach high school students broadcasting. Creating a project for my broadcasting class can sometimes be viewed as...well...from inside a teenage brain—it can be viewed as tedious. I mean there's creating the concept, writing the script, creating a storyboard, some kind of casting, scheduling a shoot, getting the gear, going to the shoot, shooting, making sure you've got everything and everybody at the shoot, composing shots, capturing the image, returning to the shop, uploading video, the *entire* edit process with graphics and sound and export to media... *and* hoping you don't need to go back and reshoot something. If you have to reshoot?—Think of the entire sequence again starting at scheduling the shoot.

Yup. It can be complicated. If you're sixteen things can go brutally wrong; or, more likely, you'll want to shortcut the thing.

Why write a script? It's all in my head.

Who really needs a tripod? I like the handheld look, it's what we wanted.

Focus? We'll fix it in post!

I've always looked at crappy projects as a natural thing. Kids are learning. Sometimes that learning includes learning what *not*

to do. I have a saying: "Bump your head and you'll learn to duck."
I can warn a team of students, "You really should write a script,"
and they'll say, "Whatevah!" I could chase them around with a
stick and make them write it...which I kind of do by making a
script a compulsory part of the project, but they'll make a crappy
one. Which is fine. Why? Because I can look at a crappy script,
warn them, let them get into production and *then*, when they
come back and ask ,"Why does our project suck?" I get to say:
"Remember when I warned you that your script was crap?" and
they can learn that a solid script leads to solid work. Bump your
head? Learn to duck.

Helping a teen follow the "Blame Chain" and finding the
root cause of their failure can be rather challenging. See, teens
want somewhere else to place the blame. Take for example an
underexposed shot. I'll ask, "Why is this shot underexposed?"
and they'll answer, "Because it was cloudy." I'll say, "Why didn't
you put the camera in manual mode and open the iris (increase
the aperture)."

And they'll say, "It's not our fault. It would have been great if
it hadn't been cloudy!" Some kids will ride that train around in
circles for hours. "Why didn't you open the iris?" "It's the clouds
fault!" It's true, weird but true, and if you have a teen you know
what I mean. Teenagers do not want to own a lot of responsibility
so they grab a hold of blame and start trying to pass it along the
"Blame Chain."

What I call the "Blame Chain" is the idea that there's plenty
of blame to go around when things go bad. Let's take our
broadcasting students and build a blame chain for them. First,
they probably didn't want to shoot on a cloudy day but they,
as kids do, procrastinated until they *had* to shoot on a cloudy
day. That's a link in the blame chain. There's a plethora of links
in a blame chain. Some are pretty weak, some are strong. Take
the cloudy day conundrum, why was it cloudy on the day they
were shooting? Because they were trapped into shooting by bad
scheduling. Rather than shoot on the first available day students
will put off a shoot until they *have* to shoot. But it's cloudy—but

kids see the clouds as the thing to blame, not their scheduling! They don't want to follow the chain to where it's anchored (themselves) they want to point at a link and say, "That's the problem—not me!"

Simply put, they want to point at the problem not the cause.

Motorcyclists do the same dang thing. Here's something that happened to me. I think it gives some insight into how we'll look to blame the links and not the anchor.

Here's a true story: Just the other day I was out for a ride with the lovely Mrs. Crash on our new ride, a Honda Shadow Phantom. As I approached a rural "Labor Camp" on a two lane rural highway I noticed a car coming the other way was slowing as he approached the driveway on my side of the road. I thought, "he's getting ready to turn in and a left turning vehicle *never* has the right-of-way."

Yep. I was actually thinking, "left turning traffic on a main artery *never* has right-of-way". Is that the stupidest thing I could ever be thinking? It was a blame chain! I was looking around and getting ready to place any blame on what was about to happen on him! He didn't have the right-of-way. If something happens it's *his* fault. Really, the only info that mattered in this situation was *"What next?"* I looked at him; he looked at me. I gently rolled off the gas and got my feet and hands in place and ready to stop.

I looked at his front wheels, which suddenly cranked left. I started braking and got ready to swerve if need be. The sudden change in my speed must have caught his attention because the front of his car dipped (on the brakes) and he stopped about one foot into my lane. With only a mild modulation in speed and a little swerve I proceeded around. No blood. No foul.

When I tell stories like this, often riders say, "If you hit him—it would have been *his* fault!"

Think about that. If I hit *him* it would have been *his* fault? Yeah, he violated my right of way *but so freakin' what?!* Mrs. Crash and I might have gotten a cool helicopter ride or been killed! Who cares who's "at fault"? If I see trouble and then plow right into it how much smarter am I than a teenager who blames a cloudy day for poor exposure?

Yeah, I *want* to get hit by a guy in a baby-blue mid '70s Monte Carlo who's going home after a hard day in the field! Financially, I'll be set forever! Think how good you'd feel laying there waiting for the medical chopper as you think: "This isn't my fault! He violated my right-of-way! I'm sure glad I didn't surrender my right-of-way! I may not be able to feel my legs but I didn't surrender my right-of-way—No Sirree!"

I worry for riders who use that mantra: the tired excuse for poor riding called "it wouldn't have been your fault." That's blaming the links. Bottom line for me? If you can see it coming. If you are anticipating having to occupy the same space at the same time as another vehicle. Adjust accordingly.

It may mean honking the horn, or speeding up, or slowing down, or changing your course. *But* if you're riding along thinking, "this is gonna be their fault," you're riding into an accident.

Grow up. Own your ride. Realize you might be in the right, but you still need to swerve. Being right and being in the ambulance?—I hear gloating during therapy doesn't make it any easier.

# DEFROSTING

Yeah, you were hoping for stories about cold-weather riding weren't you? Maybe some lusty tales of frosty adventure, visions of frozen mitts, and how nice heated hand grips are. Perhaps you expected a quick yarn about gloves or the importance of an exterior barrier layer to keep out wind and water.

Ain't gonna happen. This isn't that channel.

I'm talking defrosting the freezer. When was the last time you did that? I mean dug around amongst the hamburger, frozen peas, and carrots. Defrosting the freezer is one of those "how long can I put this off" kind of jobs; you don't do it until you absolutely have to. Last week we had to.

My nephews and nieces raise pigs for 4H. It's great for me because every year I can buy half a pig, post fair, and have it transformed into my favorite pork products. Two years ago we had half a pig transformed into nothing but Basque chorizos. Yeah. It rocked. This year we transformed half a pig into nothing but bacon, breakfast sausage, and Italian sausage. Oh happy, happy day—just don't tell the cardiologist.

The problem was that if I wanted to fit all that breakfast candy into the meat freezer I had to defrost it. Yes, we have two freezers, a meat one and a fruit and veggie one. Why? Because until August we had three sons in our house; one eighteen, one fifteen and one twelve; and they can eat. The reason there's no room for frost in the meat freezer is because there needs to be room for half a pig and a side of beef.

Besides a prodigious ability to eat, one of the problems that young men sometimes have is a certain inability to complete a task; they mow the lawn but forget to weed whack the edges or they unload the dishes but not the silverware. Often they can't figure out to put the milk in a glass before they drink it. *Or,* here's where defrosting comes in, they can't seem to close the freezer completely after getting something out of it.

That inability to completely close the freezer door results in that fuzzy, furry ice that clings to the shelves and eventually starts swallowing things up. Bad freezer ice build-up is like some strange frozen fungus that envelopes things and grows at exponential rates. You look in and say, "Hmmm, no ice," then three weeks later you look and say, "Oh, look a little ice," then two days later you look in and the ice cream is half buried, and you expect to see Burl Ives the snowman slushing around in there singing "Rudolph."

So there's lots of frost, and we need to make space for bacon by eliminating it. The process, if you've done it, is pretty simple; turn the freezer off, unload the contents into coolers, leave the freezer wide open and let nature take its course. It isn't fun; your hands get cold and you can't hold on to that frozen solid six pound chuck roast and you drop it on your toe. Oh, look, a ham the size of a basketball—where'd that come from? You finally get all the meat in the coolers and the cats figure out that "there's gold in them thar coolers!" and you start tripping on felines.

Then the waiting begins. Some folks use a blow dryer to speed things up, but I find that just letting nature take its course seems to be faster. Eventually the ice gets saturated with water and you can rub and peel it off. You need to be careful if you decide to chip at the ice because some freezers, like uprights, have cooling elements in the shelving and you can damage them. *But* you've got meat in coolers and you worry about it thawing so *be careful* if you take a screwdriver to your freezer.

Looking for the bike tie in? Here it is: drive train. I am king of ignoring my drive train. If you have a chain and sprockets like I do, you need to clean your chain, lubricate it, keep moving the rear wheel back for correct tension, watch for sprocket wear and replace them when needed, and replace the chain when it's worn out. You have to pay attention to the drive train. Belt drives can suffer from stretching and cracking so check them too. Even shaft driven bikes need attention, they contain oil that can become degraded and needs to be replaced. Check with your manufacturer for a maintenance schedule.

Why am I thinking about my chain while I'm defrosting? Cause other than squirting chain lube on the chain when it gets loud I like to ignore it. I just had to do the rear sprocket for the second time. I was noticing I need a new chain as well (and here's where we cinch the knot) but I'm putting it off as long as possible— just like defrosting. Things we don't like to do we put off. They can be strikingly important things but we'll just ignore them as long as we can because we don't want to do it.

Taxes anyone? (In a bizarre twist I actually do mine in early February...who knew?)

Dentist? When was the last time? My personal best is eight years.

Doctor? I have diabetes so I'm there every three to six months. Blood work? That I avoid but eventually get it done.

Written your will? Don't worry, you have enough stuff to do this; if you don't then who knows who'll end up with your bike? Your employer may have a life insurance payout you don't even know exists!

Need another one? Think a moment. There's something you're dreading; something you know you should do but don't want to. It can be as complex as creating a legal document or having a detailed physical exam or it can be as simple as saying you're sorry to someone.

*Third person omniscient narrator voice:*

At this point Crash e-mails this essay from work to his home so he can finish it at his leisure in the warm and friendly confines of the Crash Cave—Let us rejoin our hero, now at home.

Ahhhh fate. Irony. Karma. Ever had one of those "I had that

coming" moments? I'm on the way home and I turn down the drive at the pastoral Hacienda Crash and snick second gear for a quick shot down the lane and, "clunk RURRRRR!" happens. Pulling in the clutch, I coast to a stop and looking over my shoulder spot my chain 75 feet behind me, coiled in the dust behind me like a rattlesnake and glistening in the sun. The chain broke and then unloaded.

"*&%^!!!"

I waited too long. I won't be riding the bike to work tomorrow; gonna have to take the car and the credit card and get a new freaking chain after work. Fortunately, no damage to the bike except the plastic chain guard.

I knew it was coming. I knew it, I knew it. I just hoped I could limp it a couple more weeks until a freelance job paid off.

I stopped, picked up the chain, and performed an old school inspection; I grabbed it in the middle, stretched it out, and held it up so the flat part of the links were parallel with the ground. A good chain will have some droop in it, not a lot, and will kinda wiggle and fight in your hands. A bad chain (like mine) will droop and hang there like a sad frown. In this case both ends were just about pointing straight down at the ground. It is clearly toast and I waited way, way too long to replace it.

Did I mention that we did the big freezer defrost two days before we picked up the breakfast candy? It's natural to avoid doing the annoying, bothersome, tedious, and obvious things in life; it just happens, some things we just put off as long as we can.

The real trick is not waiting too long before we do the things we should; to take care of the detail things now instead of later. What kinds of things do we put off and what should we do? May I make a suggestion? Go call your mom or dad or grannie or gramps or son or daughter or brother or sister and tell them you love them before the chain breaks. Don't wait any longer. Don't take it for granted. Don't want until it's too late, and things are broken. Do some preventive maintenance. As for me?—Well, I'm still an idiot for waiting too long, but I'm gonna call Lil' Miss College Crash and PFC Crash right now while I'm still thinking about it.

# IMPAIRMENT

Ever ride impaired? Come on...be honest...admit... admit...a look in the dictionary gives lots of ideas. First, it's a verb, not a noun. It means to make something worse, to damage or diminish it.

Wait a moment...where's the alcohol? Why doesn't it say: Impair; to make worse with alcohol? That's because culturally we've hijacked the word to mean only one thing. In America when we talk about impairment we almost exclusively talk about alcohol; you know: booze, joy juice, rot gut, lightning in a bottle, the hard stuff, Satan's bile— whatever you call it, when we talk impairment we're talking adult beverages.

But not today. I'm not. I'm talking the pure meaning of the word. To make things worse.

Ever impair yourself? Make a situation worse? How about that time you got pulled over by that slightly pudgy cop? And you *were* speeding and he *looked* like he had one too many donuts? Did you open your yap and make the situation worse? Did you impair your driving record?

Girlfriend or wife ever ask: "How does this look?" and then

you flat out told the truth? Situation got worse? Did you impair your relationship?

When we talk about being impaired we're taking a verb and using it as a noun. Say we're out drinking tequila and we drink too much. We say, "I'm impaired," when we mean "tequila has impaired my judgment, or my ability to talk, or make relationship decisions." *Tequila* is the subject, *impaired* is the verb, and *judgment* is the object. So, when we say, "I'm impaired," what we're doing is using a *verb* to define ourselves. "I was impaired" isn't really a complete sentence. How was I impaired? What about me was made worse? When we drink our driving skills become impaired. Our judgment is impaired.

Let me tell you about the last time I rode when my operating skills and physical motor coordination were brutally impaired. Hoping for a tequila story? Nope, this is a *diabetes* story!

I ride motorcycles, and I take insulin. The danger is that when you ride, you don't want your skills or judgment impaired. Every day I get up, and I take a shot. The amount of long term, slow-release insulin I take is a judgment call. Some days, when I know I'm going to be extremely sedentary, I take a little more; days where I'll be active I take a little less. It's a judgment/gestalt kind of thing. Then, as the day progresses, I take short term insulin to process sugars that I put in my body—long story short: eat = take a shot.

If I screw up that equation then I can end up with my skills and reasoning seriously impaired. Low blood glucose levels are a lot like being drunk; you lose short term memory, motor coordination is affected, reaction times slow, judgment is impaired, and you think you're a lot better looking than you really are. (And for me?—I can get mean, curt, and ill-tempered as well.) Frankly, low blood sugar while riding is a *very* serious problem.

When my sugars are low I feel it. I know what it feels like to be low. Years ago I'd get sweaty and shake. Now I get this weird feeling at the base of my skull, like my heads floating just a little, and I get sick to my stomach. When I feel the symptoms of low blood sugar I immediately pull over and check my sugars using a small portable monitor. If I'm low I reach into my magic bag of stuff and pull out a Powerbar or other glucose booster (OK, a Snickers), relax, wait for my sugars to come back up, and check my sugars. Once they're up, off I go.

Part of this equation is being able to catch your problem early. For blood sugars 80 to 120 is normal range on the glucose index. I get below an 80 and I feel it. If I get below 60, I start thinking things like—maybe I had some bad fish, or maybe it's just too hot in here. Below 40 and I *know* I'm in a real bind. See, there's a point I get to where I'm impaired enough to trick myself into believing I don't have a problem. If I pay attention early and realize, uh-oh, I might be low, and I act quickly then there's no problem. Are there false alarms? *Yes.* Sometimes I'll pull over and check because I *think* I might be low. My mantra is to fix the problem before it is a problem, while it's still small and manageable.

It's odd, but it seems that when you're a little impaired you're willing to admit it: "I'm a little buzzed." When you're a whole lot of judgment-impaired it's easy to tell: "I'm soooo toasted." But right in the middle? Boy, you're good looking and smart. You know what I mean?

Booze and blood sugars aren't the only things that impair your judgment. Sickness, hypothermia, hyperthermia, sleep deprivation, stress, hunger—all these things can diminish your ability to make sound decisions. Here's a trick diabetes has taught me: If I think, "Man, I don't feel right," I stop, and chances are, something's probably not right. Don't wait. If you're thinking, "Man, I'm tired." You probably are and guess what? Are you thinking about *riding* or *being tired?* Hint: if you're riding along and can't stop thinking about being tired your capacity to ride has been diminished, i.e. *impaired.*

Don't take chances. If you think you might be impaired listen to your inner voice and act 'cause if you wait too long that other voice will show up, and it'll be telling you, "You're OK...

it's gonna be alright...and dang, you just keep getting better looking"; that's when you are in real trouble.

The better angels of our nature, listen to them.

# THE RABBIT HOLE

This is about a hard question: Are you afraid of your motorcycle?

Some of this may be linked to that eternal question: Why do you ride? But, essentially it's a hard and pointed question. I'm asking you to look hard into the mirror and ask yourself, "What am I?" Does riding a motorcycle thrill you or scare you, *and* do you know the difference?

For me, riding is thrilling. It's *FUN!* Not fun. All caps, bolded, italicized *FUN!* Riding is exhilarating, energizing, and sensual; it's a passion and pleasure and a release of emotion. I just love the holy heck out of it. Part of the thrill of riding is its inherent risk. You could, at any time, for any thousands of reasons be seriously harmed or killed while riding. Hell, lightning gets a couple of us every once in a while...so do heart attacks...and strokes...and staph infections...and minivans, and deer, as well as mechanical failure and human failure—they all take a toll.

That risk is a natural part of riding; some people relish it, others accept it; still others become obsessed by the danger...and by *obsessed* I don't mean high risk takers who live for the thrill of almost getting killed, I mean that small brigade that becomes safety-obsessed. They constantly clutch for the risk; living for it, I mean ruminating on it, pondering it, turning it over and over in their hands constantly looking for another "but what if?" to tack onto a situation. There are people out there that are so obsessed with the "How To" and "Safety" of riding motorcycles that I can't figure out why on earth they ride! They get sucked down the Rabbit Hole. Don't know what the Rabbit Hole is? It's that place that a certain kind of folk fall into and then, trapped in a vortex of paradox, they reach up out of it and try to pull you in.

All a person in the Rabbit Hole can see is the next twisted, hidden danger. You'll recognize those in the Rabbit Hole almost immediately. Every situation is fraught with escalating and shifting danger. As you confront one danger they'll see it as simply leading to another. Offer them a rope and they'll fret it's not a natural fiber and could stretch. Get a good hemp rope and they'll worry about getting a fiber under their nail, followed by a mean staph infection—oh and did you know natural fiber ropes aren't fireproof?

Motorcycling has a surprising amount of this sort of folks.

Every rider encounters someone who, once in a discussion runs off down the "what if" rabbit hole. You're at the burger stand, halfway through a ride, and you're talking cornering. You've got a giant chili cheese super bacon burger and you're discussing apex selection; you advocate a late apex for vision and speed selection; the other person agrees!

Staying outside and delaying the apex will give you a better sight line through the turn, they agree but, they ask, but what if there's overhanging trees and branches? What if the outside line has some sort of surface imperfection? What if there's goofy shadows, and you can't see the road surface? What if a sand dune is encroaching on the road, and light sweet crude is leaking out onto the asphalt, and Jed Clampett is standing there with a shotgun protecting his claim? What if next to the dune a large burro dropped a monstrous pile of manure on the road, and there's flies, and you go around the poo, but the flies get into your helmet, and you swallow one, and another goes up your nose, and there's a truck with running chainsaws bolted to the front of it (kinda like the ones in Avatar) and it's coming right at you with one wheel over the center line, and Jessica Alba is hitchhiking on the side of the road with a duffle bag full of DB Cooper's dough and an "I'm buying" cartoon bubble over her head—then what line should you select? (Take it, it's free—if you can't make jokes here, you're dead.)

It can be like the ole "What if?" game with a hallucinating steroid rage.

You ever run into one of those—the ones that just can't see anything but danger? It's so warped that training itself will be eschewed and mocked and you'll be told things like: "Yeah, you can take the MSF but they don't know what they're doing—they've killed tons of people in training."

I had an *epic* journey down the Rabbit Hole once. It was a digital Iliad, and online Odyssey, there were cyclops and sirens, Athena and Zeus, it was a swirling circular journey that only went deeper down the Rabbit Hole into a frightened world of "Yea, but *what if?!*"

*I just don't get it.*

I've trained people who are afraid of the motorcycle. I've counseled a couple out of riding. I've asked questions like: "How do you feel it's going?" and they say "TERRIBLE." I say, "Are you scared of the motorcycle?" and they say "YES!" and I say, "GOOD. But if you can't convert that *fear* into *respect* you're going to be frightened every time you get on it, and if you're scared, that's not good. *You* need to be in charge, not *fear*." *Fear* and *respect* are different critters.

I remember one lady who dropped the bike during the braking evaluation—automatic failure. She was unhurt. I tried to get her to *push* the bike off the range, just to show it who's boss. She couldn't. Too scared. *That* kind of fear I understand. The thing just bit you—being scared of it's OK. A dog bites you? You don't stick your hand out to pet it. In fact you might never want to be around a dog ever again. That's *fear*. *Respect* is when you realize dogs bite, and that you shouldn't extend your hand to a dog unless you can read the signs and make a reasonable guess what's gonna happen.

True story: As a young man I drove delivery trucks for a lawn/ garden/landscaping supply store. I learned to drive dump trucks and even got my semi license with that outfit. It's still in business, and the family that owns it are great people. But I'm drifting; let's get back on track. I was delivering a couple of cubic yards of supplemented top soil to a home, and as I pulled up this Heinz 57 dog was barking at me. You know, the forty pound, nondescript, could be a border collie mix, kinda of...everydog.

Getting out of the truck, I stood there and let the dog bark at me figuring somebody had to come out, right? This dog was raising holy heck, so somebody had to come out, right? After a couple of minutes I decided I'd better go knock on the door; really, this dog was barking but maybe this was it's default mode— it just barked all day and the owner ignored it.

For background: I was not then, nor am I currently frightened of dogs. They don't scare me. I *respect* dogs because they've got big teeth, but I'm not frightened of them.

I started up the walk, and the dog scurried backwards and stayed about eight feet away from me, just barking to beat the band. The dog kept his distance, he was careful not to get in boot range where I could kick him, and he kept barking his brains out. I got closer to the porch—he climbed up and stood on the lowest step and barked at me. I got closer, and he climbed to the middle step and barked at me. I took another step, and he climbed up to the top and last step and barked at me.

The next time I put my foot down it would be on the bottom step. That's when that medium sized, nothing special to remember dog jumped up on the porch, turned, faced me—and stopped barking.

My foot hovered over the step. That son of a gun hunched up his shoulders and dropped his chest about four inches closer to the porch.

I stepped back. I backed up to the truck, got in, and dumped that dirt right where I thought looked like a good spot. That dog stood on the porch and just watched me.

I was never frightened by that dog. That dog yapped at me as a warning but when the time came and he said: *"Respect me."* I did. Why? 'Cause when you back a dog into a corner, and it stops barking, it's all done talking. It's show time. There's a time for talking and a time for doing. Heinz 57 told me very clearly that we'd reached a bridge in our relationship, and he was ready to meet me in the middle of it.

Now, about the "I'm a rider but I obsess about everything that could go wrong—don't give me good advice 'cause I'll find a way to find more danger" rider—they're the dog that eternally backs up barking. They bark, "DANGER DANGER DANGER!" and when you give them a reasonable answer, they look around, as some insane caveat and bark, "DANGER DANGER DANGER." The motto the frightened rider looking for imaginary safety is: "Yea, but what if?"

It's a fear that I don't get. Can someone explain it to me? I *like* it when "what if" happens. I know that a simple basic tool bag of skills and knowledge can be adapted to fit any situation. Those guys down in the rabbit hole; they are just the ones walking backward and barking because they want *every* answer in a world of infinite possibilities. They never stop barking; they never get quiet and drop their chest, bare their teeth and get ready for the fight. The just keep barking and backing up. I just do not get it.

Me? I'd rather bark once, then turn and stand my ground and take my chances with the brains, hands, and heart God gave me.

# KEEPIN' THE RULES

Have you ever heard the term *hyper-obedience*? Generally it's used to describe what might be considered religious zealotry. Say your religion forbids alcohol, hyper-obedience would be avoiding vanilla extract. (The stuff is mandated by the government to be 70 proof!) If you are asked to pay a 10 percent tithe, hyper-obedience would push you to pay 15 percent. Why? Because for some people just doing it enough isn't! They feel compelled to do the most possible—to be more than average.

Myself, I come from what some would consider a strict religious background: no smokin', no drinkin', no cussin', no fornicatin', pay a 10% tithe; dietary restrictions, the whole deal. As a young man I had some trouble with some of those. Nowadays I'm actually pretty good at a couple—but I can still hold my own when cursing. That admission, that I have "been off the reservation" and still struggle with things, is something that I don't admit without some trepidation. When some people see failure to live to a standard, they often just see *failure*. They look for hyper-compliance, hyper-obedience—the ability to find a standard and go one better.

Example from church: I was at church one day in a meeting

and the issue of cursing came up. The obligatory discussion on "clean speech" and "filthy language" began—good stuff about clean and healthy communications, taking the name of deity in vain, and of course the value of "not being coarse." As the discussion went on, things turned to the idea of euphemisms, using a replacement word for a curse; stuff like "flip" and "frack," and how when we *say* "frack" we're really thinking something else and *thinking* it is a sin, and we shouldn't even do that.

Jeez. Really? Fetch. Things got really interesting as all this frickin' fetchin' frack was debated about how you shouldn't say "Jiminy Christmas!" because you were, in your heart, using the Lord's name in vain. Truly, it was curious. Cussing *is* bad, but that kind of hyper-obedience, I thought, was a rat-hole I wouldn't get sucked down. Yeah, right.

It turns out a couple of years ago I was working on my videos, and I found myself *seriously* debating with myself about whether or not I should wear a neck brace, you know the kind that motocross and freestyle guys wear to prevent compression and extension injures. I found myself researching them because maybe I should be wearing one on the road—to be a good example, I mean.

Wait. A neck brace for everyday riding? What kind of riding am I doing? So I took stock and I realized something—I'd slipped down the hyper-obedience slope of motorcycle safety. I had become so focused on safety that I'd started to obsess about being *the safest*. Watch my videos. Old ones will have a wheelie or stoppie thrown in for fun; or I'll illustrate a safety maneuver vividly. Watch and think about it, and you'll feel things tighten up, the fun slowly starts getting constricted, I get worried about what *other* safety professionals will think and perhaps I need to be more...more...*more safer*.

All this was followed by an epiphany moment: I was being sucked down the hole of creeping hyper-obedience. I wasn't worried about *being* safe—I was worried about *appearing* safe.

True story: There's even a weird motorcycle safety Santa story! Yeah. It turns out that every once in a while during a motorcycle club "Toy Run" someone will crash. You know what a toy run is, a couple of hundred riders strap a toy to the sled and ride down to the local shelter or hospital or orphanage and do some charitable giving. It turns out that in the world of hyper-obedient motorcycle safety that "something must be done to stop this carnage." Honest. People have conversations about how dangerous organized rides are and "when will people ever learn?" Mind you, this is a conversation that doesn't happen in the open; it happens in small cloistered groups of like-minded people. You do not debate the dangers of toy runs in the open public square— out in the open; it sounds...well...nuts. In the safety of a small group, well, then we can end up playing "safety one-upmanship." Competition comes into play; you want to be the safest guy there. The trap of hyper-obedience is worrying about what others think of what we look like, and confusing *how we look* with *who we are*.

My problem? I like to do wheelies. I like stoppies. They aren't the safest things in the world *but,* in the right place and time they're *great*. My worries about how I appeared to other safety professionals led me to a hyper-obedient state where I wasn't worried about safety—I was worried about *looking* safe. That's a big difference. I can be safe and do the occasional wheelie.

Worrying about how you appear to others is a waste of your computing power. It takes you off task and shifts your focus from the internal problem you're working on to an external, frivolous view. *Anybody* can *look* safe but isn't your energy better spent *being* safe?

# WFO

*—The following contains graphic descriptions of foolhardy motorcycle behaviors. If you find that sort of thing unsettling, avert your eyes. If you like that kind of thing? Enjoy!—*

Ever ride WFO? You know—Wide Freakin' Open—with the throttle turned to the stop? Use up all the reserves, have nothing left, all in? If you ride a bike that's making 130bhp you may have only hit the stop once or twice, there's just not enough asphalt to be constantly pinning a 600+cc sportbike. The world goes by mighty quick at 130 or more rear wheel horsepower—I know 'cause my last bike was a Suzuki GSXR1100 and going WFO could be unsettling, trees start flying by, bugs get atomized on your faceshield, and corners leap up at you like fat kids fighting for free candy bars.

Nowadays I'm riding a 40 bhp supermoto so I hit the stop a lot more. In fact just the other day I was riding with a bunch of sportbikes and, yup, I was constantly WFO. Which can be damaging to your ego when you realize "that's all she wrote" and there's no reserve, no more twist, the ponies are all running and you're just not gaining ground. Getting left behind in the straights means you have to catch up in the corners. You end up working to carry speed because conserving momentum is paramount, and you pick up your entry speed so you can pack that speed through the corner with you.

Here's a quick generational question: ever "ride the pipe"? "Riding the Pipe" isn't about surfing or skateboarding—It's a two-stroke thing—it's about getting the RPMs up high enough that you're making real horsepower. You'll often read about current four-stroke 600cc in line fours and how "to access the power" you have to rev' 'em pretty hard. Two-strokes are even more tame when they're off the powerband. Imagine a bike where, when you turn the throttle you actually ask, out loud, "Is this thing turned on?" The bike then sputters, and maybe you slip it some clutch and bring up the RPMs, and suddenly, magically, with the flip of a switch, all hell breaks loose; you're pulling yourself off the passenger seat back into the saddle, your arms are stretched, the front wheel is in the air, and your eyes are completely open.

If you know that feeling you've been on a two-stroke and you've been on "The Pipe."

Getting every bit of performance you can get out of a bike is pretty thrilling no matter what the engine design. Back in "the day" I bought a brand spanking new '83 Suzuki GS550E. Blue and white, sixteen inch front wheel, 64bhp—it would rev (GASP) to an insanely high 10,000 rpm. Most of those ponies were found above 7,000 rpm. If you wanted it to go, you had to wring it good. Fortunately I had an '81 Suzuki RM400 that had taught me to ride the pipe, so I was willing to twist it hard looking for power. One day, an off day, not a Sunday but a weekday, I was up on the thumb of the San Francisco Bay running Highway 35 from San Mateo to Saratoga—a beautiful run. You're up on the spine of the peninsula looking down over the bay and occasionally you get glimpses of the ocean. Pretty ride, good road, CalTrans takes good care of the surface—it's just a good road.

Off days on any road are fun, it's not the weekend and the roads can be very clear with little traffic. The GS550 was piped and jetted, sporting an R compound tire on the front, and I had a day off so up the road I went. I started at the north end headed south and after a couple of miles I realized a bike had started appearing in my mirrors. I actually slowed to let the rider catch me so I could get a look at it. Arriving at the first straightaway of any consequence, this 1983 Honda CB1100F just hot foots it by me.

I was not and am not the kind of guy who goes out looking for a race. However I am like a dog—if you run, I'll chase. I dropped a couple of gears and whacked it open and took off after this big Honda. We'd come up to a section of turns and I'd start catching up, and then I'd be right on his rear and the road would open up, and he'd turn it on, and I'd whack it wide open and...well, he was making close to twice the horsepower I had and there wasn't much I could do but watch him motor away and then reel him in at the next corner.

I could brake harder than he could and carry better speed through the turns yet he always walked away when the road straightened out. I passed him a couple of times, but he always motored by me in the open stuff.

The south end of 35, where it intersects with Highway 9, is pretty tight and I figured if I hustled it, I could potentially get a pass in right before the rest stop at the intersection, pull off, and declare victory—but I couldn't get it done. I climbed up his pipe, showed him the wheel, but he just held me off. I couldn't get by.

We both pulled off and stopped.

*Time out,* memory flash: There was a guy who had a yellow hot dog wagon who sold *excellent* Polishes in the turnout—I loved those things. Polish with sauerkraut and mustard...ohhhhhhhh, forbidden cholesterol goodness.

Returning to the story, his bike was all safety wired and ready to go racing, and he got off and asked me, "How do you like that 1100?" I told him, "It's a 550." He looked a little shocked and replied, "That explains the straightaways." Stories were exchanged, best wishes passed back and forth, and we went our separate ways, he back north on 35 and me south on 9.

I'm actually having a stream of consciousness thing going on here because I am having all these memories flood back. Most of the motorcycle ones tend to have WFO moments in them. Like how after my run with sportbikes the other day, I caught a Yamaha R1 and FZ1 on the Lowman Road and got past the FZ going WFO but only showed the R1 the front wheel once. We stopped for gas in the little mountain town of Garden Valley and there was a lot of peeking over the pumps and "what is that?" going on.

It's fun to run an undersized bike with the big boys. It's exciting to go Wide Freaking Open and know you're getting everything you can out of your ride. A motorcycle nearing the edge of its performance envelope becomes a living thing. They squirm and flex and wobble and breathe. You ride on the balls of your feet. You stop clutching your upshifts—just roll off, lift your foot, snap the throttle back open. This is a place beyond joyful play; it can be a terribly serious place. What was play becomes something more. Brain cells are calculating, you try to suck as much detail as you can down the optic nerves, your ears are alert and listening for feedback. The bike talks to you. It tells you "this is what this animal was bred to do." Respiration increases, your pulse increases, adrenaline flows, you become excited and flushed, and your eyes dilate.

We stop thinking about the dangers that surround us. The *passion* of riding WFO dulls our vision. *Passion* is a great word. In America we've turned it to mean *sex,* which can be a legitimate use, but in reality the word means more than that. Sex can be passionate, but passion can be more than kissing someone so hard you bruise your lip. One dictionary definition is: "boundless enthusiasm." Another is: "any powerful or compelling emotion or feeling, as love or hate." Compelling? To compel means, "to force, drive, or constrain," in other words if you compel someone you make them do something. I often feel compelled when I ride. Passion for riding can compel you to ride in a foolish manner.

Here's a definition of passion that I think can apply to being WFO: "intense, driving, or overpowering feeling or emotion; especially any violent or intense emotion that prevents reflection."

Motorcyclists caught in that passionate moment of being WFO often overestimate their skills, and forget the danger they can be to themselves or others. How can passion make us dangerous to others? By preventing us from reflecting on what we're doing. Ever had that moment of reflection after you dodged a bullet? How 'bout that time you were right between the solid yellow lines with a VW Vanagon on your right, and a Ford Capri on your left—going the opposite way? Passion can cloud the mind; in that moment I was convinced that the space between the lines was a tiny little lane just for motorcycles! Looking back at it now I just shake my head and wonder how nobody got hurt. It was an incredibly passionate and stupid moment and I dodged a bullet.

It's OK to have a passion for motorcycles and riding. It's OK to have passionate moments where you lose yourself in the thrill of riding. *But remember* going WFO is fun, but it's a passionate moment and passion turned *on* often means reason turned *off,* so be careful and don't let your passion blind you to what's going on around you—don't let that thrilling moment cloud your vision or prevent reflection.

# WHAT & WHY

Wouldn't it be great if this were a piece that explained the *What* and *Why* of motorcycles? Or *what* it is about them and *why* we like them?—Some kind of omniscient third person that explained the meaning of life and motorcycles and everything. That *would* be cool, wouldn't it? Alas, this isn't that piece. You want to know that kind of thing then you'll need to wait until you pass through to the other side, and then you can ask Vishnu or St. Peter or Odin or George Burns or whomever it is that's working the gate in your own personal vision of heaven.

Today we're talking about *What* and *Why* as concepts, not answers. When things happen, particularly if they're bad things, we tend to ask one of two questions: "What happened?' or "Why did this happen?" As standard questions they make a lot of sense. *What* tells us the particulars of the incident— generally a timeline of events and decisions, good and bad, that lead to a climactic, usually catastrophic incident. *Why* is close to the same but actually begs us to step back and look at the incident and look for conceptual errors.

As always motorcycles give us a wonderful illustration.

Motorcyclists have a propensity to crash. Depending on

who's numbers you use or trust motorcyclists are up to *twenty-seven times* more likely to be involved in an accident than someone in an automobile. That's a big number. But let's ignore it. Let's just say: motorcyclists have a knack for falling over; sometimes at speed.

It's not as fun as you might think. I've been skittering across the pavement a couple of times. Sliding, rolling, or flying over the pavement in the company of "other users" is not a pleasant experience. (Other users meaning your fellow riders or cars or trucks or some combination of all three.) Worries like getting run over or bouncing off a large moving metal object run through your head. After you have a get-off, the natural question is *"What* happened?" A detailed breakdown of who was where and what they were doing usually occurs. This is actually the timeline of an accident. Yeah, it's semantics but semantics are important. When you ask a rider *"what* happened" you're actually asking for a detailed, sequential history of the event. You'll get what you're asking for with answers like:

"I was hustling down the expressway, minding my own business, when a car suddenly dove into my lane, I hit the brakes, hit some sand or oil, and then the front tucked, and I was on my butt rolling down the road."

Getting a mildly editorialized version isn't a shock; don't we all shade a story to make us look better or taller or stronger, or less at fault. That's the reason we don't usually ask the next question: "Why did this happen?" We know *what,* but *why* is an even better question to ask. *What* simply tells us the event. *Why* reaches the next level of understanding, the place of learning. In the scenario above I know what happened: someone pulled into your lane and you crashed! It's the *why* that brings us the ability to learn from mistakes.

I teach high school. One of the most annoying things that can possibly ever happen is when you ask a question like: "What do you think of that?" and a kid answers, " It sucked." Believe me it happens.

"What did you think of that poem?" "It sucked."

"What was the effect of the Battle of Gettysburg?" "It sucked."
"What was it like for children growing up in the Depression?"
"It sucked."

You get the idea. Fortunately there's an even more concise
way to answer, "It sucked," and turn the tables. It's called *"Why?"*

Teacher : "What did you think of that poem?"

Student: "It sucked."

Teacher: *"Why?"*

Student: "Because it sucked."

Teacher: *"Why* did it suck?"

Student: "Because I didn't like it."

Teacher: *"Why* didn't you like it?"

Student: "Because I don't get it."

Teacher: "Give me an example of something in the poem
that you didn't get"

Student: "Well, the thing confused me to start with..." and
learning starts happening. Being able to explain *why* things
happen is a higher order of learning. It implies a level of mastery
of the material. *I love why.* With students, done right, it's a great
way to throw down the gauntlet and challenge them.

Back to our biker and his accident: He says: "I was hustling
down the expressway, minding my own business, when a car
suddenly dove into my lane, I hit the brakes, hit some sand or
oil, and then the front tucked, and I was on my butt rolling
down the road."

First question: Why were you "hustling"?

Answer: "I was late for a meeting, so I was in a hurry."

First learning moment: Leaving *late* and running *late* means
you're trying to make time and possibly not concentrating on
the task at hand. You're worried about being late—not about
that traffic and drivers' often bizarre antics.

Second question: "Why did a car just dive into your lane?"

Answer: "'Cause cars suck? No, really I actually might have
been in his blind spot."

Second learning moment: Parking yourself in a lane near a
car when you can't see their eyes in their mirrors means you're

probably in their blind spot. By definition, being in their blind spot means they cannot see you. (Did I mention that you're the one who decides where in the lane you park yourself and how closely you follow?)

Third Question: "So, they just jerked the wheel and 'dove' into your lane? Why?"

Answer: "Attempted murder?"

Third learning moment: Drivers may not signal, but they will do a cursory head check, they'll at least look a couple of times to make sure there isn't a car *right there* next to them. A driver that pitches a glance or two out the driver's window is looking to move over. Count on it.

Fourth Question: "Did the front slip on oil or sand."

Answer: "I don't know, maybe it was something else, but the front just locked as soon as I grabbed a big handful..."

Fourth learning moment: If you don't know what "your bike slipped on"—is it because you weren't paying attention to the road surface? Were you scanning your lane for sand and scrud, or were you thinking about how you were late and how you were going to explain it and CAR! Here's a thought: maybe he did signal and you didn't notice? Another idea: You *grabbed* a big handful. Consider maybe it was your technique.

The hard question is *"Why* did this rider crash?" That's easy: He or she was in a hurry. That's *why*. Once you are distracted, bad things can start to happen, they compile, they cascade; it goes from bad to worse to wrecked.

Ever know someone who really, really screwed up their life? Do you honestly believe that people get up in the morning and say: "Today? Today I shall completely wreck my life. This day, I shall be the complete ruination of all that I have, am, and could be. I will break the hearts of those I love, disappoint those who respect me, and do insult to those who place their trust in me."

Big problems start as little ones. They are not birthed fully formed and volatile; they start with one small bad decision that grows into a bigger bad decision, then mutates into another; they are a cancer, starting as one bad cell and then gathering and growing into something more lethal. Start telling convenient lies to your significant other about little things (client demands you go to the nudie bar) and you are on the path to telling the *big* whoppers. Ask a meth junkie! "Did you get up one morning and say—'Hey, today's the day! I'm getting hooked on Meth, that would be fun!'"

No. They probably started with beer or wine they snuck from their parents. They learned to hide the beer. Then they learned to hide the whisky, and pot, and coke, and then the meth. Along the way they learned to thieve and lie, valuable skills for addicts of anything from makeup to porn to heroin, they have destroyed their self-worth, turned the trust of others to their own advantage, and learned to lie to themselves and everyone else. Does every pilfered glass of wine lead to destruction? No! *But* every road starts somewhere, and I believe if we could see, we'd find loads of perfectly wrecked lives that started with sneaking a half glass of cheap Napa Valley red.

Now, we can track the *what* of our mythical meth addict's path of destruction but the *why* is a lot more difficult.

Not enough love? Not enough attention? Crappy parents? Poorly educated? Addictive personalities? Self medication? I don't know. Wrecking your life is a lot more complex than wrecking your motorcycle. In a bike wreck the chain of events is smaller, the timeline more focused; it's not a web of events and people.

However, there is a place where they both meet: situational awareness. Yeah, knowing what's going on around you and where it can lead. Situational awareness is a premium skill for motorcyclists; a lapse in your situational awareness can lead to amazing bursts of fear, religious conversion, possibly losing limbs, or in the worst case, your sudden, violent, gory death.

Where am I. What am I doing. What are those around me doing. They're not questions; they're statements of knowledge. If you don't have situational awareness then you're caught in a current that can take you anywhere, and anything can happen; you are a willing victim of fate, you've surrendered control of the situation to someone else...Like the guy driving the car that just "yanked it into your lane" or that guy who's been on meth for months and he's still OK.

Yeah. Why? It's shouldn't be because you turned your brain off and let someone else run the show.

# OWN IT

Ever do something that you don't want to "own up" to? Totally spaced out and blown a light or stop sign? Bought a "natural male enhancement" product? Ever buy a magazine "for a friend?" You know what I'm talking about—maybe it's an embarrassing mistake or just a guilty pleasure you keep to yourself, the kind of thing that you hope nobody sees; nothing nefarious, perhaps even something really innocent; but the kind of thing you don't want to "own."

Here's one from me: When I was a kid—I *loved* stuffed animals. I had a couple of dozen, named them all. I finally gave them away when I was sixteen and that wasn't as easy as you'd think. Yeah, being sixteen and having a bunch of stuffed animals in your closet was something you didn't want to own as a teenager. Actually, it's a little awkward right now...ahh, but if you've got a problem with it—*you* deal with it. I still like buying stuffed animals for my kids; luckily I have a daughter and you can buy a stuffed animal for a twenty year-old, and they don't mind.

Taking responsibility for our actions can be a tough business. It can require a side dish of crow. We may have to admit we did something wrong or were inattentive or innocently screwed up.

You may find me saying things like "I meant to do that!" when in fact I didn't mean to do that; I didn't intend to do that; *and* I never want to do that ever again. "I meant to do that" is a cover line used to lighten the mood after you screw up.

One of the great joys of motorcycling is taking primary responsibility for ourselves, our actions, and the consequences. That bonding of man or woman and machine, that singularity of person and responsibility, is so profound that anyone on the road will look at you and see it. Some want to be you! They see the power in grabbing the bars and saying, "This is me, this is mine, and I will take responsibility and be master of my own fate." That defiance of norm, the perception of willingness to accept huge risk and reap vast rewards is what makes little kids wave and old men pine for younger days.

What I find oddly human is that often when we screw up when we're riding, we immediately go into CYA mode, and all that responsibility we had goes right out the window! It's a natural thing, this desire to shift blame. Ask someone about that wreck they had and see how many will say: "I know I was wrong *but...*" and then add some caveat that shifts responsibility to someone or something else.

Say you are riding and it's raining. You're in a hurry to get home because you don't have rain gear with you and you're getting wet and it's unpleasant and distracting and you're pissed and cold and really want to get the heck home. So you slow a little. Not a lot, just a little. As you round that last curve toward home you feel the front start to push and suddenly WHAM! You're on the ground. You skitter across the road, fortunately unhurt, get up, pick the bike up, cuss, do the obligatory inventory of self and machine, restart, and continue on home. (Really. You don't want to spend too much time at the scene of the shame so you just pick the bike up and skedaddle—if you're lucky and fast you can clutch it and pick it up before it stalls—that saves loads of time.)

The next day your friends notice the new dings and scratches (and that little limp, too) and ask:

"What happened?"

"I fell the other day. I know I was going too fast *but* it was raining." Yeah, what's that mean? You should say: "It was raining *and* I was going too fast." The fact it was raining doesn't mitigate your poor judgment. You were going too fast for conditions, you misjudged things, you made a mistake *or* better yet, you learned a lesson! "...But it was raining" doesn't change things—this was a mistake you made.

Imagine how things would go if they ask, "Did you fall?" and you respond "I was going too fast for conditions—you need to slow a little when it rains." BINGO! You're not weaseling around looking for excuses; you're the voice of experience! Wait; that's a proper noun/title...you're the "Voice of Experience!" (Make a little echo in your head when you read that...it sounds cooler that way. "Voice of Experience...ence...ence"...come on, you know Phil Hartman could make it work.)

I recently was engaged in a virtual discussion with a gentleman who was confronted with a vehicle blocking his lane and displaying flashing red and blues. He continued forward on his motorcycle. Every single thing about this situation said, *"Stop in place."* Yet this guy tried to slip past this law enforcement vehicle. As he passed between the vehicle and a guard rail the officer ordered him to stop. Now, panicked and without a plan, our rider fell into a guard rail and damaged himself and his ride.

Yet, when you question him about it, it's everyone else's fault. The officer shouldn't have tried to stop him. The officer waited too long to flash his red and blues. The officer forced him onto a "depression era" bridge and into the dirt and grime that accumulates at the edges of such structures. The officer should have known better...

The officer? How 'bout the guy who failed to yield to flashing red and blues? How 'bout the guy who tried to sneak between a 3,000 pound vehicle and a guardrail? How 'bout the guy who forced the officer to yell, "STOP NOW!"

Everybody makes mistakes. Nobody's perfect. We lessen ourselves as riders when we look to blame someone or something else for our mistakes. We ride to "own it"; why not "own it" when it goes wrong as well? Think of the respect we have for the guy who, instead of making up excuses says, "I made a mistake. I continued forward into a constricted space when I should have stopped. If I had just stopped when the lights came on I wouldn't be bruised and scraped, my bike would still be immaculate...I made a mistake, you should learn from it."

What I'm really saying here is that one of the straight-on-sexy things about motorcycles is that they are a statement of acceptance of risk. People look at you when you're on one and think, "Man, I wish I could do that." The yearning they feel, that thing they covet, is that thing we do when we throw a leg over; that willingness to say, "This is me, this is mine, and I will take responsibility and be master of my own fate." Some call it courage. Some call it foolhardiness. Whatever it is, riding is about risk and measuring it and excepting it and dealing with it. Why take one of the truly noble aspects of riding and cheapen it with a "but..."? Be the Voice of Experience, own your actions, learn from them and let others learn from them, too!

If you're gonna ride a bike, own the whole thing; good, bad and ugly.

# BAD DREAMS

Here's the deal—I have night terrors. It's kind of interesting. Although I should have outgrown them, I still occasionally have them. According to our friends at Stanford:

What, you ask, are the symptoms of night terrors? They are sudden, violent nightmares that generally occur in the first part of the night—how bad can that be? Pretty upsetting if you're sleeping next to someone who's suffering one. And the *cool* part? If you have one, you generally don't remember what they were. You wake up scared to death with no idea why. It's shockingly easy to go back to sleep.

Ask Mrs. Crash, she's suffered through my "terrors" since we got married. It was one of those wake up in the morning and say, "Oh, yeah...I do that from time to time," things that newlyweds love. I actually had a full-on nightmare the other day, and that's what I'm going to spend some time on today.

No, I won't tell you what it was. And yes, the odds of what happened in my nightmare *really* happening are about ten million to one. Trust me, it was unpleasant, unsettling but mostly: unlikely. Which is where I want to go right now. I was listening to the news the other day, and an analyst said: "Americans like to be frightened of things that won't hurt them." Which makes a lot of sense. We worry about stranger abductions, a truly heinous and horrifying thing, something that if it happens is so awful I can't even imagine what it would be like—yet—In 1999, 115 children were taken by strangers or "slight" acquaintances. The number I've heard tossed around for 2008 is 134, but I don't have a reference other than personal conversations with educators.

Why is this important? Because as a society we truly, deeply, and profoundly worry about someone taking our children. But we don't get real excited about childhood obesity. Here's the shocker: about twenty percent of American children are overweight. That might not be so shocking until your realize that number represents a 400% increase since 1963. Woof. Imagine what would happen if we reported and worried about childhood obesity the same way we do stranger abductions. Think about it, a somber and concerned female anchor looking directly into the lens and telling you: "Today at a local high school a student had one liter of full-sugar pop, four pop tarts, and a bag of nacho Doritos for lunch. When asked about this nutritional train wreck the teen said, 'I had three of the four food groups covered; if I have a candy bar for dessert it'll be four for four.' Police have been dispatched to the child's home to further investigate."

Routinely we get local news reports, often as the *lead story*, that a stranger had spoken to a child on the way to school. Unless you're feeding your child Drane-O, as a society we pretty much don't care what you shove down their throats. We're not worried about heart disease, the physical and fiscal costs of diabetes, and other chronic diseases. We don't care if our kids grow up to be fat, soft and stupid. We don't care if they have heart disease and die at forty-five choking on a ham sandwich and cholesterol...*just as long as strangers don't talk to them.*

You're asking: "So what? What in the name of all that's holy does this have to do with motorcycles?" Here's what:

On my bike I'm deathly worried that a vehicle coming the other way, a truck or some piece of heavy equipment, will have a loose piece of equipment that will swing out and cream me. Real riding nightmare. Those big farm sprayers with the derricks that fold out like wings. I'm just sure one's going to come loose, swing into my lane, and BOOM out got the lights. Forever. It's a horror movie kind of thing; my body and the bike keep going, and...well you get the idea; the boom has razor blades mounted to it so it's a clean cut...yuck.

I didn't say it was rational! It's a fear. It's a worry. It's a thing I should be cautious of, but somehow it can consume me in the early spring when I ride. I'm looking for boom trucks that will decapitate me. Am I looking for sand and grit? Yeah, but they're not looking to give me the Marie Antoinette treatment. Am I flashing my brake light at intersections to warn the guy behind me that, "Hey, I'm here, don't park on me!"? *Yes;* unless one of those tricycle behemoths with the monster truck wheels and thirty feet of folded samurai fertilizer boom is coming the other way looking to do the Freddie Kruger to me. Honestly, sometimes I duck just before they get to me. Why? Because I have an unreasonable/reasonable fear that somehow takes over my brain.

Should I worry about oncoming traffic? Abso-freaking-lutely. Should I worry about being decapitated by boom trucks? Not so much. *But* things do fall off rigs occasionally, you say. Yes, but focusing all my limited attention on one possibility, allowing it to consume all my brain's processing power; that's just silly; human, but silly. Riders often worry about being rear ended yet in only five percent of accidents are riders hit from behind. Should you get worried about getting smacked in the back? Oh yeah, but most accidents are coming at you from the ten to two o'clock position, so a little attention up front might be wise. If you're entering an intersection worried about getting plowed from the back, you might get it in the teeth because the danger is in front and to the sides of you.

Should you worry about your child's safety? Definitely. Should you worry that the guy at the park sitting next to his bike over there eating lunch might be a pedophile using his bike as bait to snatch your child? Maybe. Odds are he isn't. It's more likely that a daily menu of deep-fried Twinkie with Oreo sprinkles is going to hurt your child more in the long run. OH CRAP! I just realized! My kids didn't have a celery tofu no mayo tuna roll on whole grain free range wheat for lunch! No biggie. They eat good meals. They had barbecued beef sandwiches. (Used some Gates sweet and mild). They also had oranges. And milk. The point is: know what to be afraid of. Pick your battles. Don't obsess. Don't let one nightmare take you off your game.

One of the blessings of night terrors is that you don't remember them. They flee at the end of the night, evaporating like spilled Koolaid on asphalt at the Fourth of July picnic. Nightmares stay with you; you relive them and ponder on them and worry about them and let them take you away from the things you really should be worried about.

Next time you ride and start thinking about your riding nightmares, the things that obsess you and make you focus on them to exclusion of all others, relax and let them go. Get some control. Focus on the real deal, the big picture and don't give up your safety for useless fear.

# Keeping Time

Ever watch a "talent" based reality show? You know, "American Idol" or "America's Got Laryngitis" or whatever, and some poor sap gets up and starts belting it out—and stinks! Yeah, that's why I watch, too. Some get their hearts broken and I feel bad, others are truly befuddled that they stink; it just hasn't entered their minds that *they stink*.

How does that happen? What fundamental wiring is missing in their heads that they can't understand that they (to twist a bike term) sound like a scalded cat? Is it nature? *Or* perhaps nurture? Stay with me here; I'm going into the human mind and that's a frightening cesspool of dreams, rainbows, and rotten unicorns so this could get weird in that not-so-fun way.

First, I've been around enough teenagers with iPods plugged directly in heads to know this: snug some earbuds into your ears tight enough, turn the volume up loud enough, and guess what?—*You sound great!* You sound exactly like: Mariah Carey or Iggy Pop; whomever you have turned up to 11 and is damaging your hearing. The fact is, once you can't hear yourself anymore you sound *great*. Think about it. You're parking a 747 at a jetway and you're bored, so you take off your ear protection and start belting out show tunes. You'll sound *exactly* like Liza Minnelli or Robert Goulet or Regis for that matter. If you can't hear you, then you sound good. That explains self-delusion. But what about all those who say, "My friends say I'm *great*," or, "My Nana says I'm the greatest ever! And she dated Al Jolson!"

It could be Nana is deaf as a post or lying about that speakeasy with the Jazz Singer, *or* she might be your Nana and she will think anything you do is fab. (Come on, you made a ashtray in kindergarten that she treated like it was the next "David"—she's biased, OK?)

So what makes people say overly kind things to bad singers, besides kindly human nature? Remember an ugly baby is never called ugly...to the parents.

I believe the problem that gives bad singers hope is that they can "keep pace." Keeping pace is a thing we do on motorcycles. A group leaves. The alpha rider gets to the front, either by preplanning and consensus, or by brute force; every group of riders has a leader. He may be the guy who we all vote goes first or he may be the guy who can get his gear on fastest or he may just be one of those guys who works his way up front by passing everybody on the road—but there's a leader to every group. By default a large group that commonly rides together will designate the "fast guy" or "fast gal" as the leader. Again, it may be for safety *from* the leader (you don't want them passing everybody) or because the leader is the safest (most experienced, most skillful). Sometimes a leader will be smooth and calm, setting a pace that is comfortable and fun; other leaders are riding hell-bent-for-leather, and you are taking your life in your hands trying to keep up.

When I say, "keeping pace," I mean that you can ride with the leader without getting yourself shoved into the hurt locker. Keeping pace means you can ride with the fast ones when they're cruising along and are putting a moderate amount of coal on the fire. You can keep up. Your timing is right. You follow their lines and brake when you see them brake and accelerate when you see them accelerate. You keep up.

Here's where the tricky part comes: just because you can keep pace doesn't mean that you're a good rider. Yeah, it's weird. Ever hear of a "guide track"? Singers will use them to keep themselves on key and on time during a recording or performance. They will, literally, sing along with a pre-recorded track of the part they are singing. This is *not* lip-synching; this is having a voice in your ear singing that you sing along with.

What? You've never heard of this? It happens. Can you imagine the world of hurt you would be in if, say, you were on a nationally televised television show and your voice failed and your guide track (also used to bolster your potentially weak voice) were suddenly heard on air? You were singing with your guide track, and the guide track is filling out your voice and making you sound great, and *you* stop singing. It'll keep singing without you. Production trick: How to make a live show sound better? Use a guide track.

Keeping this all in mind, imagine a rider who's been "keeping pace," just running along fat, dumb, and happy behind the fast folks who suddenly decides: *"I am fast.* Every ride, they realize, I ride with the fast guys. I am fast. I should lead. I should be alpha dog."

What do you think's gonna happen? The same thing that happens to folks who, after years of singing along with Prince with the headphones, decide to belt it out in front of a group of seasoned professionals who know what good really sounds like.

A person who can keep pace, who's adept at following, will get themselves into a world of hurt when suddenly *they* have to decide when to slow, what line to take, where to accelerate, when to pick it up or slow it down. They can follow the guide track that's always been in front of them but when that comforting companion of good, solid, well paced, on key leadership is gone, so is everything else.

True story: After you leave Boise and get way up on Idaho Highway 21 headed to Stanley you'll arrive at the little village of Lowman. Lowman straddles the South Fork of the Payette River. As you cross the river you can continue up Highway 21 to Stanley *or* you can turn left and go to Garden Valley, then on to Banks, and then down to Boise again.

One day as I'm rolling into Lowman I see two bikes turning left onto the Lowman/Banks Road. From the looks of them, one's a sportbike and the other is some kind of standard. I think to myself, *"Ooh, Look. Motorcycles! Catch them!"* I don't know why but I love to find other motorcycles and ride with them. I'll leave for a ride by myself and then seek out other riders to run with.

Pouring on a little steam I hustle a bit and shortly am getting close enough to recognize what the bikes are. One is a Yamaha R1—a 1000cc, inline four cylinder sportbike that puts 160 or more horsepower to the ground—a bit of a monster; the other is a Yamaha FZ1 which has the same engine but is tuned to be more "rider friendly." I, on the other hand, am riding on a single cylinder 400cc half dirtbike/half streetbike called a supermoto. It's a little like a beagle (me, hyper, small) looking to play with a wolf.

My options are either push them, let them go, or keep pace. A quick inquiry with my high school teachers would probably get you a consensus opinion that I'm a bit of a knucklehead. The good news is that I'm smarter now than I was then. I decided to pace these guys. Just to see what they had, you know, gentle curiosity.

As always, once they realized I was behind them they did exactly what I would have done—they picked up the pace. No insane wheelies and disappearing into the distance, they simply picked up the pace. Things started going by faster. Realizing that I could never keep up with the straight line speed of these monster inline 4s I decided to pick up my pace in the turns. I was braking later, carrying more speed, trying to make up for lack of horsepower with "flowpower"—carrying as much speed as I could.

One truly strange thing that happens in situations like this is that you catch people *in* a curve. As they slow earlier and more, you stay on the throttle longer and brake less, and the feeling is pretty strange to be catching up to someone *in* a turn. It's a dangerous situation! And I'm starting to run up the FZ1's tailpipe in a couple of turns, and he knows it. It's at this point that he makes a profoundly wise decision; that decision that can be so difficult for anyone to make.

He decided to slow down. Moving to the right side of the lane he waved me by with his left hand. Our "pace" wasn't right for him anymore, he was outside his comfort zone and simply said, "Enough," and waved me by. Brilliant. The kind of thing I have trouble with. Did I take the cue?

*Of course not.* I'm a knucklehead. Do the smart, prudent, reasonable thing? Who you kidding? I started reeling in the R1, that race based, fire breathing, snarling beast that goes 85 mph in first gear and still has five left. By the time we hit the big straightaway by the Fire Attack Heliport and he turned the throttle, I knew I was wasting my time. There was no chance of keeping up. In fact the guy behind me caught back up, and I waved him by. The brutal truth is my bike will go 104 mph, downhill, with the wind at my back...if I didn't eat a big lunch. The R1 will do 185 and still have some headroom.

I was in a situation where I couldn't keep pace anymore, and trying to was foolish, and...well, I didn't see how it could end well. (*Plus* the lovely town of Garden Valley was coming up quick and getting a 100+ ticket in a 35 seemed like a bad, bad idea).

The challenge, as I see it, is to be able to understand who, where, and what you are. In your riding or your singing are you "keeping pace" or are you truly gifted? Are you fooling yourself about your potential? Are you realistic and rational?

Here's an example of how we can misread *"keeping pace"* and what it means. I teach video production at a high school. We actually service three schools—students from all the schools in the district come in take my class. One of the really cool things we do is we make highlight videos for all the schools' major sports. Generally we have a football and a basketball reel for each school. We make wrestling highlight reels, occasionally lacrosse, soccer, girls hoops—we try to get a lot done so students have a keepsake from their high school career *and* we get to do a little fundraising.

Occasionally we have a parent call and ask for all the highlights we have of their child so they can send them out to coaches and try and get their athlete a scholarship. Which is great—we'll take care of you. It's good for my students and it's good for your child, so why not?

Here's the hard part: occasionally I have to tell a parent, "We don't have any highlights of your child. He's second string, he never plays, and the one we do have of him—he fumbles." Tough business that. Junior may be a great kid. He can keep pace with the team, but he isn't a college prospect.

A second string fullback isn't going to be a D1 running back. An R1 will always outrun my bike. Mariah Carey *is* a better singer than ninety-nine percent of the country. Just because you're on the field, or the road, or can sing along with someone doesn't mean you've got chops. You may be able keep pace, but you're not on the same plain. Or is it "same plane"? Never mind—the issue is that you should accept who you are, be comfortable in your own skin, and don't do something stupid trying to prove you're something you're not. Why? Why not reach for the stars? Isn't desire enough?

*No.* Wanting it isn't enough. One of the great dangers in motorcycling is when the pace gets too fast, and we don't have what it takes to wave the guy behind us past. We want more than we can deliver. Understanding our shortcomings *and* our possibilities are vitally important parts of self-awareness. *I am not saying quit.* I am saying accept who you are.

But here's the cool part. I may want to go 140 mph and run with the R1s on my scooter *but it will never do that.* Not possible. Put me on a twisty 40 mph road, and I'll eat them alive. Bottom line? Keeping pace isn't bad, it's OK to be the second string fullback. Be the best second stringer you can be. Build your heart, learn discipline, enjoy being part of a team, but don't delude yourself that keeping pace with something, makes you a titan at it. Know who you are and enjoy being that.

You may not be a great football player, but you can be a hell of a teammate if you know when to wave the next guy around you.

# FLOW

I bought a big ole HDTV at the beginning of the year, just in time for the Super Bowl. Yeah, it looked good. I also bought the BBC documentaries "Blue Planet" and "Planet Earth" at the same time. I had heard they were was beautiful and entertaining and informative so I saw that they were bundled together; it was a good price and I bought them.

Woof. Beautiful! We watched "Blue Planet" two hours a night, every night until we had seen it all. I grew up within an hour of the ocean and had always ridden my motorcycles to the beach, so I grew particularly nostalgic as I watched. I also spent a summer working in Hawaii and snorkeling occasionally, so I really was able to access some long forgotten memories about the ocean and how pleasant just being in tropical water can be. My kids were just blown away by the scope and beauty of things, but I was sucked in, feeling things I had forgotten, remembering times and places and smells that I had put on the back of the shelf for a long time. Ever hear a song for the first time in ten years and suddenly you're transported back to that perfect summer day you had as a teen? In your mind your best friend is next to you; you're both young and the memory glows like embers in your mind and

115

you can feel the warmth of the day and you just feel good. Yeah, you know what I mean.

We moved on to "Planet Earth" and, never having been to Africa and other points exotic, I was back on the same plane as my kids. Just overwhelmed by the immensity and complexity of life and how beautifully it had been captured. At some point pictures of antelope and such were being shown. Excellent stuff captured from a helicopter, tracking shots that allowed you to see the flow of the animals. Somehow each animal was running alone; yet all of them were running together like a great furry river. The herd seemed to flow like some taupe river casting off dust instead of spray! The herd flowed away from predators, around bushes and trees, over imperfections in the landscape, and the camera followed it all seamlessly.

I realized I was watching something I had felt before, something that I had been part of. I looked at my kids and they were watching but not transfixed as I was. I was connected to the video in a way that they were not. Herd footage, when animals are running sinuously and leaping over the landscape, clearly speaks to me in a different way than it does my children. I pondered a long time why I connected with those images. I realize now it's for two reasons.

One is Frisco, the first horse I ever owned. I was, what? thirty-five when I bought him. I didn't grow up around horses—except to deliver hay for a garden supply outfit I worked for. We used to fight about delivering hay because, where I grew up, hay meant horses and horses meant two things: money and girls. Where I grew up, horses were a luxury item—generally kept by girls. You know, "Daddy? Can I have a horse?" To teenaged Crash, horses were a way to meet rich girls and get paid at the same time.

Later I married into a ranch family. I moved to a small farm. Then I learned about horses. I learned to ride. I learned to load and unload them, to saddle, curry, neck rein—the whole deal. We bought Mrs. Crash a horse. We got horse-poor, which is just like motorcycle-poor—money just starts flowing that way and disappearing.

Right after we started buying horses we took them with us to the family homestead out in the desert to help roundup and brand cows. After branding we went for a ride with three or four other riders. At some point we got into a big horse race—just running like hell. I don't know the proper terminology, but when a horse moves from a canter/trot to a full-out gallop something very special happens. You float. The horse becomes this low ellipse that you're on top of, you just float there in a gentle cycle of up and down; the other horses move around you and you through them and this mystic living dream of animals and riders just... flows over the landscape. You forget to be frightened and are just thrilled to be in that place where you're not a rider in the control sense—you're an extension of the animal, and you become a part of it; you sense where it's going and what it's going to do before it does, and there's a perfection of symbiosis that melds you into the horse. If you've been there you know what I mean.

'Those were the memories I was connecting to as I watched those antelope run. I had run—had flowed—and when I saw it, I felt it.

Now, I realize that those feelings of being part of the liquid herd are not just from horseback; they come when you run with other motorcycles. It doesn't have to be ten or twelve other bikes, just a couple of good friends you trust; the kind of folks that you don't mind being a foot or two away from; seesawing closer and then farther away. Nothing crazy mind you, just that feeling of being in the flow. If you've been there you know what I mean. Back in the day I used to—aw heck, call it what it is—I used to street race up in the Santa Cruz Mountains. Just strafed 84 and 92, Bean Hollow, Pescadero Road, Old Page Mill Road...and if you found someone to run with, or a couple of someones to run with, you'd get in that loping, flowing wolf pack that just burned up the road (and endangered everyone on it). Mystic? Yes. Dangerous? Oh yes, very.

*Attention: please observe all posted speed limits and road regulations.*

I've seen that same pack running in World Superbike or

MotoGP. That's part of the allure of the spectacle—watching the herd stream around the track at impossible speeds with that mercurial grace and flow. Just like watching antelope, I sit up, lean in, and breathe a little harder than the people around me.

I have been in the pack, the herd, the school; it's one of the most magical, beautiful feelings you can have on a motorcycle; running with another creature like yourself, thoroughbreds, galloping beasts breathing side by side, flowing with and down the road. Looking back at it now, I should have been on a track somewhere. It's a miracle no one got killed.

The *flow* is a liquid thing and being part of it is a beautiful feeling. You should enjoy it when you're there; but you don't have to be going 100 miles an hour to feel it. You can feel it at the posted legal speed limit—and if you exceed that limit?—I understand, sometimes the blood gets pumping; but remember: bad things can happen in fast moving herds—pay attention during that documentary and you'll see that occasionally one of those antelope trips and falls, and the lions catch it. Sometimes when the antelope falls, he takes others with him.

Wanna know the difference between antelope and us?—Have you ever seen a herd of antelope stop, mill around a moment and then ask, "Where's Steve?" then say, "OH SH*T!" and go back looking for him?

That sense of flow, that feeling of being part of the sinewy herd, yet being completely alone; of being part of something, yet still being someone, is part of what makes riding so fantastic. Enjoy the flow; just remember there's a time and place for everything. If you find the flow is getting fast, especially if it's getting stupid fast, then it's time to join the fast pack and take it to the track!

# FURNITURE

Ever sit on a bad couch? I mean one of those *"Holy crap! This is like a prostate exam gone bad!"* couches? And the owner looks at you and says, "Don't you just love it? I looooove that couch!" LIAR! Or maybe they were some kind of masochistic freak. Or maybe they're looking for something different in their couch than you are. It's hard to tell. I like my couch medium firm. Leather is nice because it warms up to your body temperature and helps you fall asleep. Yes, I like to sleep on the couch. The couch is my friend, my ally, my mistress. I go to the couch to relax, to slip into a favorite place, and be comfortable. Couches should be stain resistant, so I can spill stuff on them. I'm six foot tall so loveseats are out; a couch needs to be long enough for me to lay out full length.

Couches should be able to double as beds *but never BE a bed.* "Hide-a-beds" are really "wreck-a-couches." You can't settle into a couch that has a full size bed wadded up inside it; it's like trying to stick a hamburger patty in the middle of cherry Danish and call it a "hide-a-burger"*—It's either one or the other!*

Not that I've got anything against multitasking.

Here's where motorcycles and couches cross at the corner of

"What Is It?" and "What Does It Do?" Streets. Right now I ride a supermotard, or supermoto, which is kind of a dirtbike with streetbike wheels. (Go Google it, that'll make my life easier.) When people ask me to explain it, I often say things like "it's slow in the fast stuff, and fast in the slow stuff" or "it's the slappy good fun—I just smile when I ride it." It won't go more that 100 mph, and the seat is a torture device, but I *looooove* it.

It's a vehicle that is just plain fun to ride.

When I ride it, it's mentally comfortable; I can get to that place where life and riding become hand in glove, things just happen the way I want them too. My bike is my couch, it feels right, it goes where I want to go and does what I want it to do.

Choosing furniture and choosing bikes have a lot in common. When I started to think about moving from sportbikes to motards I was very careful about what I was doing. I was literally redecorating my riding family room. The couch is the central fixture of a good family room. A wrong couch can devastate a room, absolutely ruining the aesthetics of the place; the function—the livability—can be destroyed. It took me a long time to make the move to buy a 'tard and once I did, I hung on to my Suzuki GSXR sportbike just in case. The poor Gixxer sat in the garage so long the battery went flat. Selling it wasn't easy, it was like getting rid of that perfect couch; even if you found a new perfect, it's hard to let go of the old.

If we're working the couch metaphor, let's explore a couple of other areas it's very applicable. Here's one: Who ya gonna let sit on your couch? Think about it. Who would you invite over for pizza and red Hawaiian Punch (the kind that really stains)? 10 year-olds? Near your puuuuuurfect couch? With a permanent stain in a cup waiting to happen? What about some nice hoity-toity wine tasters? With good red wines. You know, nerds with attitude and little money to back it up; the kind that make grand sweeeeeping gestures with a glass full of merlot? You got the right bike for you, do you have the right people with whom to share it?

Choosing riding companions is a tough business. Not so tough to start, come on, I'm *not* inviting the Harper Valley Pre-

School Artists Club into my family room; those finger painting nut jobs aren't getting anywhere near my couch. I sleep on that couch; I don't want it smelling like preschoolers, urine, and paste. My couch is special, and I don't want anyone "special" doing anything "special" on my baby. Initially sorting out the pre-school set makes things easier. In fact, no teens either. And college students; they're out too. Sloppy people—no sloppy people; *or* mechanics fresh from work. Or butchers, unless they clean up first; don't come from the killing floor straight to my house. I don't have anything against butchers or mechanics; I'm just anti-dirt-on-my-couch.

We can go on! I don't want painters right after work. Or weightlifters after a workout. No sweaty football *or* basketball players. New rule: Everybody who sits on my couch or gets near it will be freshly bathed, carefully coiffed, and *not* have body odor.

I'm not picky though.

Or am I? Should I be? I mean, really, if you're gonna ride your motorcycle, your baby, your place of comfort and peace, shouldn't you be careful who you let near it (and you)?

Let us use a dirty word: discrimination. Take a deep breath. Let me show you a positive usage of this word: I am discriminating in my choice of riding companions.

Meaning I am: discerning, selective, judicious, astute, and tasteful in my choice of riding companions.

For me a riding companion should:

1. Have the same goals I have for the ride—enjoyment, safety, exhilaration, and camaraderie. A ride with another person is a social event, not a competition or exhibition.

2. Be willing to allow for my mistakes and strengths. I should be able to go as slow or as fast as I want and not be ridiculed for it.

3. Be willing to bail out. No, not crash but willing to say, "Hey, you know what? This ain't working for me, head on without me. I'll catch you some other time." The ability to recognize you're in the wrong place at the wrong time with the wrong person and be willing to rectify it is woefully missing in America today.

4. Still be a friend after the ride. (See above)

Bottom line? Be discriminating. Choose your ride and your riding companions carefully. Choose your couches carefully. Nothings worse than being saddled with the wrong couch, it's embarrassing, costly, and difficult to fix. *And remember,* we all look for different things in our couches, but that doesn't mean we don't love them. I sat on this Swedish thing once that I think doubled as a torture device in the Middle-Ages. I hated it. The owner loved it. Everybody at the party loved it. I didn't start a fight about how wretched the damn thing was. I just stood. It's not *my* couch, I got nothing invested in it, I don't *have* to sit in it. See, getting along isn't hard, start by being discriminating in what you buy and where you sit. If you see a couch you don't like, be discriminating in what you say.

Standing isn't hard. Biting your tongue is.

# RERUNS

Like them or hate them, reruns are part of life. Recently I was on a plane with those seatback TVs, you know the ones with the screen above the fold down tray, and I swiped my credit card and coughed up the 4 bucks and started to watch TV at 40,000 feet. Which was cool...until I realized I'd seen a bunch of the shows that were on, meaning instead of having a gallon of gas in my scooter, I had the same "Ace of Cakes" I had watched on the way *out* of Kansas City as I had on the way *into* Kansas City. "Silence of the Lambs" was on too but there's only so much cannibalism/serial killer/bureaucratic incompetence/saved by innocent ####### I can stand to watch. And did you realize that SportsCenter on ESPN, if you watch it for more than one hour, just recycles—*reruns*—the same highlights and stories?

Yup, it's true.

Eventually I found a "Deadliest Catch" I had seen before (there's a storm on the Bering Sea and the waves are gi-freaking-normous) and I settled in to watch all the guys I know do the things I expect and barely make it out alive, just like they did the last time I watched it; *and* I liked it.

All this treading the same ground got me to thinking about

my favorite roads. I have favorite roads I love to ride. To be exact, I have favorite sections of favorite roads. Places you really commit to memory, you burn them into your brain, and you know what they're like according to the particular time of year or weather. You name your favorite sections of a road; private names you may or may not share with other riders. I have my own "carousel," there's "switchback city," and there's a little section of Idaho 21 I just call "high and tight" which includes a spot named "Dan's Corner" and another called "Sara's Corner." Why name corners? Because I've been there enough to feel some ownership, some connection that lets me claim it as "my road" or my "section" of a road. Something may have happened there *or* I just decide in Crash World that I'm giving a corner a name to anchor it in my mind.

On my plane ride I was chaperoning teenagers to a national technical skills competition. I've been able to attend this competition four years in a row now because my students have been SkillsUSA State Champions in Video Production for four years. I've gotten to know Kansas City pretty well—but only parts of it. Food Network has helped open my horizons as I try to get to places I've seen on shows. I follow the path set for me by people who've been there before. Likewise, my students trust me to show them cool things in KC. I've taken to asking for help on internet motorcycle forums—trust me—want good advice on where to eat or what to see, ask bikers; it works. Find someone who's seen the show, and they can tell you where the good stuff is and when to change channels.

As I was spending my week with teens, we had an interesting conversation one day. It when like this:

"Mr. Crash?"

"Yes, Jane?" (Names have been changed to protect the innocent.)

"Have you heard about Sally's new boyfriend?"

"No. Do I want to?"

"YES! She's eighteen and he's twenty-nine!" (GASP!)

"That's not fair," I said.

"Fair? What do you mean that's not fair?" I confused them. I like confusing them; or maybe confounding is a better word. I like confounding them.

I went on to explain that when a twenty-nine year old man is dating an eighteen year old girl he is at a distinct advantage in the relationship. He's been there before. He's done that before. It's a rerun to him. He can gauge where the relationship is going and guide it because he's run the road before. The corners aren't a surprise to him. He knows that there's shade in a corner until eleven am and in that shade, if it's been cool the night before, there's a chance of water and less traction, and he knows to slow down. Knowledge of the road, understanding the terrain, can give you a tremendous advantage.

Think of your favorite road. Visualize your favorite turn. See it? Good. Then if I were to show up behind you on that road, coming up to that turn, who holds the edge? Who has the advantage?

Every road has someone who "owns" it. Someone who, every week, comes up and carves it; they learn the road, they love the road, and they "own" the road. They pass cars in places they know they can get away with it by timing it just right. Speed trap? They know it. Gravel spills into a corner?—They know where. Got a mountain spring weeping at the end of blind turn?—They know when it stops running in the summer.

Sometimes a road's "owner" will use that information to their own advantage. Ever been hustled by someone who knows a road? Ever hustled anyone? I'm talking about gently suckering them in, getting their speed up a little, and then BANG you're at the "flip flop" in the "chicane," and you look back to see them completely screw up and cross the line and scare the pee out of themselves. You evil bastard! But they deserved it, it is your road... and they shouldn't ride over their heads...and if they're dumb enough to try and push you on your road, don't they get what they deserve?

We don't often think in the black-and-white world of experience, and advantage and disadvantage. Eighteen year old girls don't think, "He's twenty-nine, he might know how eighteen year old girls think. He might be able to manipulate me or drive me into situations I'm not used to and put me in a place where I might do things I normally wouldn't do." Fathers think that way, mothers too. They think about the unfair advantage that experience brings. Parents worry that their child is in a situation where they could be taken advantage of and hurt.

Do you think about that rider behind you, the guy who answered the call on a local forum for "spirited ride"? I'm not saying ride their motorcycle for them; I'm saying is your ego just big enough that on your road you use your experience to feed your own ego? Do you take the advantage? I know it's hep and cool to say, "Hey, on a motorcycle you're on your own," but shouldn't we be careful *not* to use that as an excuse to lever our experience against another rider?

Honestly, couldn't the world use a few more people looking out for each other a little bit more? You don't have to ride their bike for them, but maybe, just maybe, we should take the chance to slow down a little and teach them the road—not teach them a lesson.

# CALM LEADERSHIP

I went for a ride today and learned, or relearned, an important lesson. On today's ride we went up to Moores Creek Summit and were debating about continuing on around to Lowman and Garden Valley. Frankly, I sissied out. It was cold. We were looking *into* the clouds. There was snow on the sides of the road, and I flat out wussied it up and said, "I'm going back to Idaho City. The sun is shining down there." My chest was starting to get cold... insert NancyBoy excuse here...and there was sand on the road— yeah that's it.

Anyway, after my sissy-itis started catching and everyone decided to return the way we came, someone said, "Watch out for the section of road with the 'Trucks Entering Roadway' signs; it looked really, really dirty going the other way." We all nodded and agreed that "yup, it looked ugly" and then reminded each other, "There's rocks and crap in the other lane too, it's the uphill side"; and wise motorcyclists that we are, we took off back down the hill.

I'm old. Almost fifty. Who knew? But the beauty of this situation is that I can be slow. I get to be the last guy in line. I've got the most gray in my beard and I can call "sweeper" and nobody argues. Naturally, I was last in line; three bikes in front of me; me hustling to keep up.

As we went down the hill we came to a sign saying, "Trucks Entering the Roadway," and I thought, "OK, be careful." My pea-sized brain said "slow down" and I did. It's just that the road wasn't as bad as I thought it was going to be. It was relatively clean. It looked a lot dirtier going the other way, I thought, and I rolled back on to catch up.

A couple of minutes later we got to another temporary diamond sign about trucks. And we leaned into a right and the road went all to hell. *Dust, grime, scum* was all over the road—you couldn't see the asphalt! I'm not talking a little, I'm talking *a lot,* twenty or thirty yards of crap coming off of logging/earth moving/support vehicles getting dumped and dragged from a new dirt road out onto the paved surface.

Fortunately for me I had three decent riders in front of me. Nobody freaked; no one grabbed a big handful of brakes, or chopped the throttle; no urine came flowing out of anyone's pant leg...they just rode through it. I had enough time to brake while still on good pavement and then got off the brakes and rode through the crud. I honestly cannot remember seeing *anyone* in front of me brake, probably because they had done the same thing—braked when they could, rode on through.

See, that's the thing to remember. You know how they tell pilots, "No matter what happens—keep flying the plane"? Riding is just like that—no matter what happens. Keep riding the bike. Inexperienced riders will do things like chop the throttle while on a sketchy surface, and that unsettles the bike; or they'll keep on braking hard in the marbles and just throw it away. Keeping cool when you're in a tight spot is paramount in getting through a squirrelly patch. If traction is at a premium, then doing a ton of traction-consuming actions can be a bad, bad plan.

Here's why it's terribly important to have a good leader on a group ride. Our little group had "Linker33" in the lead—he's a skilled rider, which is good! Why? Because he could have binned us all! How? By wadding his bike. If he hadn't been smooth and calm in a tight spot then every rider behind him suddenly goes from "tight spot—keep on keepin' on" to "OH CRAP! HE CRASHED! I GUESS I WILL TOO!" Once the lead goes down, so do the hopes of every rider behind him. Rider #1 crashes and everyone else *expects* to. It's easy for riders to watch the first go down, and then they go from riding to crashing in about 1/20th of a second. Why?

Because you're trying to avoid hitting the rider sliding down the road in front of you. You've just been presented with absolute proof that doing what you're doing can result in crashing *and* you're suddenly off task—you're not riding, you're witness to an accident. It's hard to look past the tumbling bike and rider and then keep riding your own bike. (If you've been there you know what I'm talking about).

All of which brings us to selecting who you ride with and who you get behind. Yeah, put a guy on point who can't keep his wits, and you're gonna regret it. That's not to say that, on any given day, a quality rider won't have a brainfade and make a mistake—it means that if you decide to follow a squid, squidly things will happen. Do yourself a favor when you ride *and* in your life; put a wise, experienced person out front; they won't freak in a tight spot. I don't care if it's business, or church, or politics, or what— put a knucklehead out front, and knucklehead things will happen.

Thank you, Kris, for not freaking out *and* for reminding me to keep my wits about me.

# FAST TALKERS

Ever find yourself in the break room at work, fridge door open, trying to decide whose lunch to steal and start listening to the conversations around you? You'll hear weird stuff. People talk about everything from how to cure foot odor to how to fool your insurance agent (What? Did I leave the RR off that Honda CBR1000 application? Oopsie!)

One thing I hate is listening to that guy who's reeeeeeeally good at something. He'll be telling his "I'm a righteous golfer" story—the one where he out drives John Daly or chips better than Tiger Woods, and you'll be listening, thinking, "I should call BS on that one," and before you can, he's running his mouth about how in high school he was "a contender" but was knocked down by mono the week of the qualifier...got it from the girl who was almost Miss Teen California by the way, she was totally into him, like crazy-stalker-girl into him...blah, Blah, BLAH.

I hate that guy. I always want to hand them a club and say: *"Put up or shut up."* Guys like that spend a lot of time trying to convince us of how good they are. Ever wonder why that is? I have a theory: they're trying to convince themselves. Deep down they understand that they're just a decent weekend hack and it bothers them. They want to be more, so they start convincing themselves that they are. Suddenly that mediocre high school golf career becomes the glory that almost was. Remember that time on the back nine at the public course when you hit that long putt? For these kinds of guys that putt, instead of being a one-off, becomes a mental daily occurrence. They relive it soooo much that it becomes common in their heads and presto, every hole was that way.

Deep down something nags at them—oh wait—the *truth* nags at them, and they suppress it by telling their story over and over, embellishing it, polishing it, creating mirrors and shadows that create an army of hot golfing goodness. To borrow a seventh grade cliché: they become legends in their own minds.

We got those guys in motorcycling, too. Down at the shop they'll tell you how fast they are. How they rip it up on their bike—"Sometimes I can only stretch that GP A tire 4000 miles before it's toast," "I was down at Palomar and slapped a wicked pass on this slow Yamaha, turns out it was Jamie Hacking out with Jay Leno," "I was gonna club race but those guys are so slow it's dangerous..."

You know *that* guy. There's one at the bar, or the shop, or at the turn out. You've met him *and,* if you're a knucklehead, you've gone riding with him. How'd that turn out by the way? Ambulance? Tow Truck? Stupid story about how the bike's not working right?

The problem with asking someone to "put up" is that in lots of situations it's amusing to watch. In others it's just plain dangerous. Take our fast talkin' golfer for example. You're headfirst in the fridge; you find a good looking pastrami sandwich so you're feeling your oats, so you pull your head out and say something like: "Dude, we should hit the links sometime. What are you doing Saturday?" *If,* and that's a big *if,* if the guy is smart he'll make some excuse. *If* he isn't he'll take you up on your offer. Then on the course you'll be treated to hours of good fun with excuses like:

"These aren't my clubs, mine are in getting resurfaced..." or "Usually I play with a balata, but my girl gave me these crappy balls for Christmas..." or "I pulled a groin the other day, just ain't all here..." hack, slice, splash. You hear a lot of new and exciting excuses which is fine and fun because very, very rarely are people killed on the golf course because of another golfer's ineptitude. (I would say *never* but there's got to be an exception to every rule.)

Motorcycles, on the other hand, are an entirely different issue. When you invite a fast talker on a ride you're entering a space where 500 pound motorcycles are moving at 75 to 150 feet *per second,* and if one guy screws up, he can take everyone with him.

I mean honestly—where's the danger in golfing? Standing inside the arc of someone else's swing? "Well, you see, I was trying to see what kind of ball he was playin', so I leaned in and WHAM he swung—I never saw it coming. Lost seven teeth and my sense of smell."

Conversely, an overconfident motorcyclist who's in over their head can spear you from behind or lowside into you while they're pulling a bone-head pass. They can smear themselves down a guardrail *or* kill a family in a minivan head on. There's just way too much bad that can happen when you give someone the "put up or shut up" when it comes to bikes. If someone is spending all their time telling you how fast they are—stay away from them. Going for a ride with them only means you're placing yourself in a situation where they can prove their incompetence and kill you at the same time.

Back where I come from we had a saying: "If someone spends all their time telling you how fast they are? They aren't." The trick is to let them be fast in the parking lot and stay away from them in the twisties. It's just easier to let someone prattle on than it is to try and put the pieces back together once they've proved themselves stupid.

There is a flip side to this whole thing. Remember the "for every action, an equal and opposite reaction?" Yea, the guys

who never talk about how fast they are. You know that guy—
his bike was a little worn but mechanically sound? He wasn't as
fashionable as most. He never talked about makin' that crazy ass
pass on that SUV. Remember him?

Dude *was* fast wasn't he? Smooth too. Don't get suckered in,
let the fast talkers talk—ignore them, let it go; anyone who has
to spend their time convincing themselves of how good they are
is probably a danger to be running with. Look for that guy who
just likes to talk bikes, he's the guy who can probably teach us
something.

"Did I mention what a great writer I am? Yeah, they asked me
to move to Idaho because Hemingway used to hang out here and
they could use a little literary shot in the arm...Ever been to a
bullfight? Blah, blah, blah..."

# TEACHERS

I think it's safe by now to figure that you know I teach high school. Today I shall share with you some survival secrets of teaching which, oddly, flow over into motorcycling. As a teacher, every once in a while you come across *that* student. You know, that student, the one that can learn but for some reason won't. Maybe they're not trying, maybe you're trying, maybe there's some visceral reason they won't listen or you can't reach them.

They're just *that* student. They just won't learn. Everything about them says they should, but they just don't. Every once in a while they *do* get it done, and they do it well, and you think—why can't they do this more? Smart, charismatic, capable—but just can't get it done with any consistency. Alternately they break your heart and then make your day; and in the end, they just come up short. (Wait. I think I may have been one of these... grrr...Stupid payback.)

Some of you are going to be very, very disappointed in what I'm about to say, and I do not blame you. I also offer that until you've swam up crap creek for a couple of years, please withhold judgment. There are situations in life where you have

135

to say: "Ain't been there, don't know what I'd do." The student you just can't reach is one of them. If you haven't lived it, you don't know it. Are you a parent? Then you may have lived this, too, and if you have, you may have come to the same place. That place, that evil, painful, sorrow filled, well of despair is found down at the end of "I've Tried Everything" Lane in a special circle of surrender called: "The world will beat it into, or out of, them."

Yes, it's dreadful. Yes, it's shocking. And yes, it happens. Why? Because every once in a while you have to say, "I've done as much as I can do," and move to the next patient. Simply obsessing on fixing one student can end up damaging all the students through neglect. ( Remember the part where I warned you disappointment was looming? We're here now.)

We teachers talk. It's a social group. We hang out, we worry about stuff like students, and we'll ask peers, "What about so-and-so? He's dying on the vine in my class, I can't seem to reach him; lights are on, somebody's home, but when you ring the doorbell he answers the phone." This subset of students we're talking about is a strange one because they'll check out of one class but still get it done in another. That lack of uniform behavior can make you nuts. In all honesty, more often than not I'm on the lucky side of this equation; kids struggle in other classes but not mine. I teach Broadcasting! How hard is it to hold their attention? They all want to be Spielberg or Cameron or Tarentino. All I have to do is channel that energy. For the most part, I get to be the lucky one saying, "They do great in my class."

But not always; and Lord it is frustrating when a kid who could, who *should* perform doesn't; so we pass the buck. If it's a bad habit or attitude: "The world will beat it out of them." If it's a needed skill (often social competencies like knowing when to say what, and when to shut up) then guess what?: "The world will beat it into them."

I can teach good sense. I really, really can! Bad news is—I can't guarantee you a child will learn it. I can preach, cajole, lecture, assess for retention, all that good teacher stuff, but the kid who thinks that it's his first amendment right to throw the F-bomb?—He'll take the detentions; he'll take the suspensions, and eventually, he'll stop—but he'll *believe* he's oppressed and that boy, when he gets out in the real world, he's sure he'll be vindicated. Surely his boss at the Burger Barn won't care if he throws the F-bomb in front of the customers. It's his first amendment right. The ACLU will step in and defend him right? How do you help a kid ditch a belief—a closely held, hopeful, willing to take a bullet for belief? How do you shake that? He'll comply with the rules, but he'll tell everyone he is being crushed under a fascist regime. Acting on knowledge to avoid penalty these kind of students won't assimilate the knowledge. If knowledge could be pushed into your head, injected into your brain, that's how we'd do it! The bitter truth is (and maybe it's a bitter beauty) some kids just won't, can't, or don't get it.

Sadly, kids can be their own worst enemies, and even a great teacher can't get them out of their own way. Hanging in the teacher's lounge we'll just turn up our palms and say: "Let the world teach it to them." Yet as much as we feel we failed to get that key bit of social competency into a kid, we just need to believe they'll somehow, someway, someday get it.

Which lands us at that theory that "The world will beat it out of him"; that enlightenment won't happen in the academic world but will come in the brutal pounding of the "real world." Working at your best friend's "car detailing" business might not be the real world, but it will come; reality and awareness are out there lurking like pimps at the bus station, wolves waiting to chew on the weak and inexperienced. The moment will come when the world steps in with a mallet and strikes them on the head and says: "GET IT?" In my little delusional world I see a picture where, in their pain they'll think "Oh, *that's* what he was trying to warn me about!" (Revenge fantasy? Maybe. Or maybe just a daydream of vindication.)

Here's the bike tie in: ever run into that rider who just

doesn't get it? At the turnout or drive-in he's the one walking around with the "Helmets kill, you're better off without one?" stories and the "Right before you hit a car, jump up in the air and fly over it! You'll be OK!" (Neglecting to point out that if you had enough Flying Wallenda in you to be able to pull this acrobatic stunt off, you'd be flying through the air at 30 mph, leading with your helmetless head!)

You've met this guy. Imagine having him in a motorcycle safety class! They're not bad people. They're just...knuckleheads, and they *believe* what they spout. Like motorcycling's jailhouse lawyers, they take some odd physics, hang a few warped facts on them, ladle on a big serving of "sounds right" and "I knew a guy who's cousin's hairdresser's nephew..." and PRESTO! "You should never use the front brake, because the bike will flip right over!" (Why not jump off ala the big collision avoidance plan?) *Or* from another camp: "You should never use the rear brake, you'll just skid and highside." (A true issue, but not an axiom. Rear brakes can be your buddy—especially depending on the style of bike you're riding.)

Like my students, these are *not* bad people; just misguided. Somewhere, out there in Cyberville, there's terabytes of give and take with this sort of folk. Out in the bar or garage right now there's someone shaking their head and asking friends, "When is he gonna learn?" Just like in the teacher's lounge, riders will say: "They're gonna learn the hard way, and I don't want to be there when it happens."

I'm betting this is not the first time you've heard these. As riders we often shun knuckleheads as dangerous, we invent ways to distance ourselves so we "don't have to clean up the mess." We hand our problems off to "The Road." The Road will teach them the error of their ways. The Road will punch them in the face, and *then* they'll understand. The Road is a hard master.

Consider now the idea that the world won't beat it out of them. Imagine the Road never rises up to trip them and teach them.

That would suck. No righteous vindication? No standing in the hospital saying, "I told you so." What about that moment when, stopping at the end of the off ramp the guy holding the squeegee and paper towel looks through the windshield and says: "I should have listened to you in class—Steve over there is selling oranges—do you want one?"

No "I told you so"? Don't be a buzzkill! I was counting on that as part of the retirement package.

Fearing for the safety of the misguided isn't wrong. In polite society we have a duty to help knuckleheads, to help people see the error of their ways—that's why it's so dang annoying when folks don't listen. Part of the social contract is help each other; in that big human herd we're supposed to help each other out, point out danger, share wisdom, and guide others through the wire. That's why when someone absolutely won't learn—we eventually shrug it off and "let the world beat it out of them"; because we want them to learn the lesson with the pain that can accompany it. Why don't we "want to be there when it happens?" Because we don't like seeing those we care for and love pay the price for an inability to internalize or assimilate a simple idea or rule.

Teachers care for students. We love our friends. No one wants to see people damaged, emotionally, physically, or economically because they just won't listen. The joy and pain of high school is that the knuckleheads naturally move on. Wait four years and the odds of seeing them again drop to near zero. I occasionally see students after graduation but, honestly, it's rare. I have no need to see a kid that's failing in life. I don't want to. I like seeing bright, successful young adults who are launched on the road of life and flush with excitement and hope and possibilities.

What's my point? In the long run, in your heart, you don't want the Road to teach anybody any lessons. You're just afraid it will, and you will be left with someone you care for who is bruised, broken, and in pain. Guess what? You're human. You see someone you care about heading down what sure looks like a bad path, and you turn your head and look away. You're normal.

The real world problem is that your riding buddy's never going to graduate. After four years at high school, eventually we'll ask you to leave. You're not friends for life with the brick and mortar of your school. The challenge in the "Real World" isn't waiting for the Road to teach your friend a lesson—the challenge is to stay on the Road with them and help them learn to avoid the potholes and find the right line.

High school students *have* to leave me behind. You get to continue the journey with your friends; treat 'em right.

# TIRES

Quick! Think of all the names you've heard for tires. Donuts, buns (sticky or regular), meat (as in street meat vs. dirt), rubber (got some new rubber), sticky bits (British guy confused me), skins, even gatorbacks (shucked caps—you know the tread of a truck tire lying in your lane looking like an alligator).

We may use different language or dialects, but we're all talking about tires. I love my tires. I'm a brand-loyal guy. Once I find a tire I like, it's difficult for me to change. I've been riding the same flavor tires for years and years. I *trust* my tires and by extension my tire manufacturer. I've been changing brands and it's been hard; in fact I haven't completely made the switch yet; I'm still running my ole favorite on the front and "testing" another flavor on the rear. Habits are hard to change.

Tires are one of those things we tend to ignore. We place our faith in them and expect them to be like a trusted dog, always there, always friendly, always ready. Come on, when was the last time you broke out your tire gauge and checked your pressures? Generally, I ride every day, and old truck driver I am, I simply hit the tire and listen for the tone. *If* things don't sound right, I check. If Saturday or Sunday is a ride day, then I check pressure the night before.

Tire pressure is important. Too much can stress the tire to a point of danger; making the bike overly sensitive to steering input, as well as creating the potential for catastrophic failure due to pressure and impact. Not enough makes the bike sluggish and slow to respond, as well as risking the tire popping off the bead of the rim—which is why checking pressure regularly is important.

Carelessness happens, and we can forget to check. "I mean really, I checked last week and the week before and the pressure isn't down. Why bother? I thumped it, and it sounds good..."

You're expecting the terrible tire story now aren't you? The "I didn't check my tires and now I'm sorry" part. Ain't gonna happen.

I will admit my tires are shot. I was giving them the once over and the rear *and* the front are as close to the wear bars as you can be, and not be there. In case you don't know you find "wear bars" in the grooves of your tires in four or more spots in the middle and sides. Simple idea really, as the tire wears away rubber is shed and the tire itself loses mass. (Physics guys don't hate me, I'm not doing math here, just talking about the loss of material from the tire, so excuse me if I'm not using pure terms here). As the tire sheds rubber and wears down, eventually the surface of the tire scrubs down to the wear bars and once the wear bars and the tire's surface are at the same level—*it's time to get new tires.*

I would suggest ordering tires *before* you reach the wear bars. Going beyond the wear bars presents odd little problems like the tire footprint changes dramatically as the tread pattern disappears, you can chunk the tire out (the tire's rubber thins, starts to fall apart, losing chunks of rubber), or steel belts or plies start showing through, all very bad things.

The part of the tire that is pressed to the pavement is called the "contact patch." A motorcycle's contact patch is very, very small if you compare it to a car. Go out in the garage and look. I'll wait. Kinda spooky, huh? That's OK though, 'cuz you trust those tires don't you? I mean you check them for defects, pressure, and all that stuff every time you ride...

Tires are what ground us. They are a fundamental survival issue. Good tires in good repair are the foundation for optimum use of available traction. Yes, I know there's lots of physics we can talk about, but let's not. Let's focus on the idea that if you go out on a shagged tire, you're immediately putting yourself at a disadvantage, as your contact patch is no longer working for you well as it could. Your most elemental connection with the ground is compromised before you do anything. That's nuts. Have you looked at your tires lately? Really looked? For road damage? Did that pot hole tear a chunk out? Is there a roofing nail in there? Where are the wear bars?

Now let's take this idea of something very, very important that we simply assume is going to be there and in good shape and apply it to something fun...like sleeping! Right now it's 0100 hours. Yep, one in the morning. We have a couple of wiener dogs, and one is snoring right now. I'm jealous. I'd rather be snoring right now. The youngest in the Crash Clan, Fender Bender, got a hamster for his birthday, and it's turning hot laps on the hamster wheel right now. How do I know? It puts chew toys on the wheel and then runs, and it sounds like a tennis shoe in a dryer.

That's not what's keeping me up. I'm worried about work. That, and I need to cut hay next week, and then I need a week without rain so it'll dry, then we have to bale and stack it. The biggest Crash kid? The six-foot-three, 230 pounder? He's 2,500 miles away now, so he can't help *and* he's an undersized starting offensive lineman and that's dangerous...

I could pile tons on here, but let's face it—we all got things that keep us awake at night; worries that nibble on our heads once we hit the pillow. My goal here isn't to get you worried about the things in your life that keep you up at night. My goal is to make you aware that you are up at night. Every night may not be a night of angst, but you may pull a double shift at work, or stay up too late watching the Olympics, or you sneak out to a movie, or just get hooked in a good book, but we all lose sleep here and there.

Sure, I fret, but I also had this great idea I had to get out of my head and onto the page. It's OK to get short changed on sleep; it happens to just about everyone. The real question is: are you aware of it? Is it happening all the time? Have you got used to it and just live with it? Is it like your tires? Do you just look at it and say, "Yeah, it's OK"?

Just like tires, we'll overlook sleep until we come to an event where we really need it. Lots of college kids stay up late the night before finals, but as we get wiser we realize it's more important to go to bed early before that big presentation. We want to be "fresh" for that important job interview or well rested for that round of golf with the boss. We worry about sleep when we know something big is coming. You want weird? I have diabetes, and I actually worry about looking tired for my regular checkups, so I hit the sack early the night before.

Do you hit the hay early before that big Sunday ride? Do you check your mental and physical air pressure, tire condition, and wear bars before a rip up the canyon? Are you ready for the morning commute on your bike with 10,000 sleepy goofballs in cars?

Me? I have to teach teenagers about "Radio as Entertainment" tomorrow morning; we get to listen to Orson Welles and talk about "watching" radio. Bottom line: I need to sign off and get some sleep, with luck I won't be too bleary eyed, and maybe I'll drive the car instead of ride.

Damn hamster wheel.

# KARMA

If you're reading this you're at least interested in motorcycles, which is important, because I want you to remember what it's like to be with a group of *non*-motorcyclists. Imagine you're in the lunch or break room and you're the only one who rides. It's possible. The cheap television sitting on top of the soda machine is running some kind of newscast and you notice above the anchors shoulder a little motorcycle helmet and some kind of police tape or something that visually says: *Motorcycle Story*.

Fortunately, there's a remote standing next to the TV and you say to him, "Steve-O, turn that up!" Steve the accountant is pleased with this new cool nickname, so he reaches up and cranks up the volume. The anchor reads:

"Sheriff's deputies say the motorcyclist was splitting lanes and riding erratically before losing control of his motorcycle and striking a parked car. Paramedics pronounced him dead at the scene. No word on if alcohol was involved but deputies tell us the victim was not wearing a helmet."

Now, and this takes imagination, what if the news anchor turned to their co-anchor and said, "Should have been wearing a helmet; sounds like he got what he deserved!" How fast would you be on the phone? Where do you send the first e-mail? What forums will you post in? Can you make it to the "Fire Fred the Unfriendly Anchor" rally that will happen next week? Are you ready to ride around and around the station revving your engine?

Now imagine the same situation differently. The anchors blather a moment and pitch it to the weatherman. Sitting in her corner of the break room, Tina from Shipping says: "That guy got what he deserved."

"Pardon?" You say.

"That guy on the bike," Tina replies, "I mean really, if you ride without a helmet, you get what you deserve."

What do you do? It's a tough spot. America's getting to be a pretty rough place, a "sow the wind, reap the whirlwind" kind of place. It is true that he knew the risks.

So you listen a moment and say, "Bikes are dangerous, but so is eating pizza or operating a crane. Anytime anyone gets killed, not matter what or how it's a tragedy for someone." Then you gather up your half-eaten lunch because you're not hungry any more because someone's husband or father or boyfriend or brother or child won't be coming home, and that's a tragedy anyway you cut it. Everyone looks at you askew, because you just threw water on their chance to grind on some loser without a helmet. You mumble something about having to make a call, and you slip out.

There is another choice: you can hang out and join in. This is your chance to be king. You can be right. They know you ride, whatever you say will carry some weight. You're the expert! It's fun to be the expert. You read somewhere that the number one fatal injury to motorcyclists is striking the back of their heads on the pavement, so you talk about the importance of helmets.

"Then you're an *idiot* if you ride without a helmet," Tina says.

"Gotta protect your most valuable assets," quips Steve-O; "I bet they were wearing chaps!"

Big laugh. It's inappropriate and you know it, but you can't help yourself, and you kick in: "Motorcycling is a dangerous business— you buy your ticket, you take your chances."

"Yep," says someone, "they got what they asked for—they got what they deserved."

Ever done that? *No?* Not even in a forum? Online, where nobody ever really knows who you are? Really? I have. I admit it. In the public privacy of being online, I have been a jerk. Haven't we all?

It's OK though, the motorcycling family occasionally breaks down. We become fractured, and like that moment in the break room we forget who and what we are. Online it seems to be worse; we're not just trying to hide in a group, but we become part of that anonymous voice that isn't accountable for what it says.

We can be ruthless, even cruel. We laugh as cosmic justice deals out its hard reward.

Stunter dies on freeway?—"Got what he deserved."

Cruiser goes wide, hits tree?—"Shouldn't try to ride fast on those things, shoulda bought a sportbike."

Girl falls off back of bike, skin grafts needed?—"ATGATT Baby; live and learn."

First time rider dies coming home from shop where he just bought the bike?—"Idiot should have got some training."

Then after posting and applauding all this cruelty imagine you're on your ride home one day, and you let your eyes drop. You start thinking about something, anything, maybe its taxes or bad judging at the Olympics, and you're not focused on riding anymore. Suddenly there's a minivan left-turning in front of you! How did you miss that? Didn't they signal? It wasn't there a second ago!

You grab a big handful of brake and, since you weren't scanning enough, you didn't notice the diesel stain on the road, and the front tucks, and you get spit right into the van. You hear that cracking noise that you can feel...and there goes the rear tire of the van! Damn, that was close! You must have hit the front quarter panel and bounced off! At least they didn't run you over.

Then it's quiet, it's always quiet after a crash, the world stops. Mentally, you decide to do a systems check (that cracking sound wasn't good—you felt it). You wiggle your fingers.

And they don't.

And your feet won't wiggle.

You must be stunned; it'll come back; you got zinged, and you're just numb.

Your hearing starts to return. Someone's screaming and crying. Sounds like kids from the minivan. You try to turn your head but it won't go—a face appears in your field of vision, just a normal guy in a Corona shirt positioned in the center of your face. He speaks:

"I'm a certified EMT. Don't try to move. Can you hear me? Are you having trouble breathing?"

Sirens, firemen, cops, crying children, there's a backboard, someone's cradling your head, you can feel that and the oxygen mask, and somewhere a woman keeps crying and saying, "I never saw him, I never saw him." She's completely hysterical, you can hear her babies crying for their Mommy. I never saw him!" the crying mother sobs.

Then a male voice answers, deep and comforting, "Its OK ma'am, motorcycling is a dangerous business, you buy your ticket, and you take your chances. I'm sure he knows the risk."

It's never fun to hear your own words used against you.

Someone once taught me if you want to give justice be ready to receive justice.

You want mercy? Then you need to be merciful.

Come on Ladies and Gentlemen, motorcycling is a sport and a passion, a lifestyle that's full of good people who make bad choices, and some who just have bad luck. Should we turn our backs and mock them, or reach out with a little mercy? Nobody's perfect... and if you are, are you really the kind that throws stones? Next time you hear about some poor biker who does something stupid give them a break. They made a mistake; maybe they didn't know better or maybe they knew better but just bet the wrong horse on the wrong day.

Karma. Do unto others. You get what you give, nobody wants what they deserve.

Maybe it's time to give a little kindness—heaven knows you may need it someday.

# Play

Do you ever play? I mean *play,* let yourself fall into that childish exuberant place where you're experiencing extended joy? Giggly good fun? There are times when adults can play—like, yeah, it *is* a puzzle, when do *we* play? It seems to be kind of against the rules when you get past eighteen. We get in our own way and don't want to look stupid, or other people tell us, "Adults don't act like that," and we cave and surrender to being all grown up. In the long run it's kind of sad that we leave that part of ourselves behind and forget or refuse to play.

Do you remember when you used to play tag? Good old fashioned "You're it!" tag on the playground or out on the school yard? I do. I remember going all out playing tag; that pure exhaustion, complete surrender to the game; the kind of moment when you knew Mom has gonna bust your chops for getting grass stains on your good "school jeans," but you just didn't care, and you just went for it. Those are delicious childhood memories whether it was an endorphin rush or just overloading of the juvenile nervous system with sensory input and strategic calculation.

It was just the pleasure of play. Getting older meant fewer

moments of pure abandon and play; as we progress to adulthood we begin to expect and admire things like "self control," "maturity." and finally (and I believe this can be a sin) we cherish "acting like an adult." As we age we slowly close ourselves up so no one can see our blissful abandons, and then we forget how to enjoy them. Frankly, we get boring.

Play has several symptoms, clues that tell us we are entering that zone of release. Our pulse quickens. We become flush. There can be light-headedness. We smile, then grin, and laugh, and the air tastes good, and we access that center of ourselves. A Zen thing happens, and we are in a state of play, of euphoria, of childlike joy.

Often I find myself in that rapturous state when I ride motorcycles. Let me share a couple of occasions with you:

First—Motorcycle Tag. Have you ever played this? It's a dirt bike game where you define a field with inbounds and out of bounds (preferably small—under 1000 feet square—so you can't get up too much speed), first or second gear only, *any* contact is considered a tag. One guy is *it* and off you go. If you're *it,* and you bump your tire into someone's swing arm—they're *it.* You can literally reach out and touch them as you go by. Stick a leg out and give a solid push to the seat?—They're *it.* This is old fashioned tag, as we played it as children. At some point as we played this we became kids—thrilled, joyful, laughing children on dirt bikes chasing and dodging and scheming and *playing.* We had the joy of play. Oddly, no one ever got hurt. (I actually play ATV tag with Mrs. Crash, and she giggles and shrieks like a schoolgirl when we do—it's a beautiful sound from a beautiful girl).

Second, Parking Lot Practice (PLP). This is that informal practice we do on our own in empty parking lots. I would argue that good parking lot practice is actually Parking Lot *Play.* The other day I went down to the local high school, where I know they teach the Idaho STAR beginner course. I got there right as the lunch break started. We're talking about a couple of acres of cordoned off asphalt, free of cars or obstructions. Knowing the right people pays off, and the instructors were kind enough to let me "practice" in this open "safe" area. (By the by, high school parking lots seem to be just about dead empty early on Sunday mornings.) So I started puttering around and practicing my full lock rights and lefts, and my weaves and braking. I was all self-conscious, because some students were sitting around eating, but as I rode, the tires warmed, and I loosened up and started to *play*. I just played. There is no other word for it. Joy. Riding. Me and the bike. The bike and I. Play. Pretty soon I was weaving through the cones that line the range. I started hitting thirty-five and practicing my emergency stops. The world closed down, and it was me, the bike, and the asphalt. I was fully in the moment.

Finally I realized I had no idea what time it was, my bubble of attention opened, and I looked up, and most of the class was back sitting on the grass watching me. Remember when you were a kid and you were fully engrossed in play, and your parent or teacher snuck up and watched you, and suddenly you sheepishly realized they were there? Yeah. That happened. I rode over to the instructors and said, "Clutch is your buddy! Thanks," and kinda slunk off. Play—adults don't do that. Oh well, *I* do.

I could go on about the bike and how the roads you learn become your friends; or the people who you ride with and how, when you trust them, you get to the place of play in your riding—that place where you're in the flow together and it's just blissful and clear and beautiful.

There is another time that we as adults can play, a time when we can be exuberant, loud, goofy and even ridiculous: when we're around small children. It's true. Ever play peek-a-boo with your union rep? Or the UPS guy? Or the cop asking for your license? Of course not—you'd end up getting tasered and spending seventy-two hours in observation. But children are different. I was sitting in church the other day, and yes, God looks out for fools and small children but, as a fool, I'm hedging my bets and I go to church, where I often encounter small children in the pew in front of me. They get bored and stand up and turn around to get a look at the rest of the congregation and, well, what's a guy to do? The ensuing festival of making faces and peek-a-boo madness is really the definition of goofy adult. I believe it's embarrassing for everyone in the Crash Clan, however, I cannot help it. It just happens. Making children smile is a blessing reserved for more than just clowns—trust me, try it, it's worth it.

What's today's lesson? It's really quite simple: *play*. Find a way to shake off the adult for a few moments. Short sheet the kid's bed. Put a frog in the silverware drawer. Crank call your wife/husband/ girl/boyfriend/son or daughter at home or work. (I send the text message "BZZZZZZZZZZZZZZZZZZZZZZZ" and when they text back, "what are u doing," I send back, "bugging you.") Climb a tree. Reach across the table in the lunchroom and tap Steve-O's hand and say, "Tag—You're it!" Have a race at dinner and see who can eat the mashed potatoes fastest. Throw the mashed potatoes. Have ice cream for dinner. I don't know, just find something! Turn up the radio or computer and dance with your significant other. Tickle. Stick your tongue out. Fly a kite. Find that thing and that person that makes your heart beat faster, puts a flush in your cheeks, and makes the air taste good, and just let it happen!

It's gonna be different for every one of us but please, unchain your inner child, they've been imprisoned long enough—go, PLAY!

# THE TALK

Everyone who rides has received it, usually without asking; often from people whose only qualification to give it is, well, they have an opinion. Generally, those who offer it don't much know you, your circumstance, or experiences. Simply because you ride and they have an opinion they feel entitled to share it with you. Seldom solicited, often condescending, full of myth, legends, and lies—let us talk about "The Talk".

I have received "The Talk" from: my mother, father, brothers, mother and father-in-law, brothers and sisters-in-law, pastor, coworkers, complete strangers, a drunk guy who couldn't walk, a drunk girl who cried—"Tinkers, Tailors, Soldiers, Sailors"; heck; I've got it from all kinds. Having been exposed so many times I'm actually fairly immune. I can actually look the person in the eye, nod appreciatively, grunt, "You've got a point," all the while not listening to a word that person is saying. To be honest, those that give "The Talk" deserve a break; you should assume good-intent. If they feel the need to warn you about "how dangerous those things are" they're probably good-hearted people. They don't wish you evil, rather they wish you to avoid it. *You* might be a proxy for the person to whom they wish they had given "The Talk."

153

People who are willing to approach you at the gas pump to give you "The Talk" are true believers. They aren't approaching you because it's a whim—it's a calling. It's one thing to give you a scolding across a turkey at a family gathering, but it's another story to walk up to someone you don't know and...well...give them the business.

Remember, when you're getting "The Talk" you'll know it. Some folks try to back into it; they ask about the bike, how long you've been riding, the weather, then they slip into, "I know a guy who had a friend..." and it's off to the bit on organ donors and "donor-cycles." Grisly stories of collecting boots with feet still inside might be told, descriptions of feeding tubes, paralysis, weeping, wailing, and gnashing of teeth can follow.

I don't mind. Why? Because these are well-intended people. They're scared—scared enough for you that they feel compelled to action. Talking to you isn't an option, it is something they *must* do. The word *catharsis* comes to mind. From the dictionary, catharsis is:

"The purging of the emotions or relieving of emotional tensions, esp. through certain kinds of art, as tragedy or music."

When a stranger comes up to you and tells you to "be careful" they may be vomiting up a fear or a warning they have wanted to release for years. Imagine if you wanted to warn a friend but didn't—and now you've got nowhere to put that counsel; you pack it around for years and then you see someone on a bike and something about them reminds you of a lost friend; here's your chance, all you have to do is walk over...

To me. And guess what? It's OK. I don't mind. Why? Because your heart is probably in the right place. And yes; nosey, know-it-all, obnoxious, pushy, annoying people give me "The Talk" but I just let it go; why let them ruin my day? A miserable, unhappy person is looking to make other people miserable and unhappy; nothing is more fun than denying a bitter, angry person the pleasure of creating another.

The point? If someone's trying to save you, listen, be polite, and say thank you because life is too short to be offended by the well-intended.

# Doing the Hard Thing

Everyone at sometime, somewhere, will be faced with doing the hard thing; that thing you just suck it up and do. It might be a brave and noble thing that requires self sacrifice. It might be the mundane chore that no one will do that has to be done. This sort of thing ranges from taking the flashlight and going out into a nasty storm to fetch the dog or having to walk up to a friend and tell them that they've lost a loved one. As I said, everything from the mundane to the triumphant to the tragic. Some stuff just has to get done and sometimes you're the person who has to do it.

You'll know it when you're staring it down. In your heart you'll feel that resignation that, "I'm gonna have to be the one." It's nobody's fault; some stuff just has to get done and sometimes, *you're* the one to do it. Example: Child vomits in the car. You get the child home, he or she wants the other parent (come on, it's gonna be Mom) and you, the papa, end up standing on the porch, looking at the car and thinking:

"Somebody's got to clean that up!"

You know it's you. Inside waits a slightly processed hamburger and fries, some strawberry shake, and pre-chewed Gummi Bears. Gross. But that's the beauty of some situations—you know what you have to do. There's no getting around it. You might not like it, but you know it's you or no one. You take a breath, mentally steel yourself, step up to the plate, and as the pitcher lets go you turn toward the catcher so the ball hits you in the back. You've had to take one for the team, and it felt OK, you know?

Here's one from the Crash Files: Every religion has customs for how they deal with death and funerals. I'm part of a tradition where family, or close family friends, dress the dead for burial. It's something I've worked very, very hard to avoid. We have a lay priesthood and I've been in leadership positions (Go on, laugh, it's OK.) and I've always managed to *offer* to help but not been needed. Half of life is knowing when to open your mouth, the other half is knowing when to shut it.

When my pop passed away, our family gathered around my mom, and we worked on getting things taken care of. Pop's death came at the end of a long downhill slide with heart disease and it wasn't a surprise to anyone. He knew it was coming; his affairs were in order. We knew it was coming and had prepared ourselves for it. We had made lots of trips to see him to make sure the kids got time with him, we had been videotaping and sending edited pieces to him to see the kids at work and play. We had just done our best to be prepared for what was to come.

Except me, because I'm a knucklehead. I *thought* I was ready. I was planning on dedicating the grave and being a pallbearer with my brothers, sons, and nephews. I was ready to stand in a receiving line at the viewing and do all those things. I even went with my brother and mom down to the funeral home and proofed the programs for the service.

I was not ready for when my mom turned to me and said, "You'll go down with Bishop Keller and dress your father?" It was one of those question/statement things where you realize that, yeah, you are going do that for your mom. You might not want to do it, but it's the honorable thing. You've never done it before in your life, but you can because your mom just asked you to do something, and she asked *you*, not somebody else.

The hard thing can be dirty or uncomfortable or awkward but it has to be done, and there are lots of different levels of intensity of the hard thing. It ranges from changing a diaper to holding someone's hand as they pass away. If you're a doctor you might have to tell someone they have cancer. Accountants have to tell people they're broke. Mechanics have to give good people the bad news about the GTO, or hand over a bill they know someone can't pay. A teacher may have to tell you that your kid is...well...more than special; he or she is diagnosable. Someone has to pick up the garbage, sort through the waste, reach into the dark, cold, slimy place. Out there, in the next 24 hours, someone has to tell someone, "Dude, seriously, you need to bathe more."

In motorcycling there are hard things that have to be done. Like many of life's hard things, they're generally not physical things—they lean to the mental. Want a tough motorcycle job? Go be an Instructor. Watch and coach and hope and cajole and then realize you're going to have to tell someone, "You're a danger to yourself and others. You need to go home." Break a few hearts, for their own good. You get to cushion it. You can say, "Today's not your day," and "Maybe you should ride a bicycle and scooters—scooters don't have a clutch." As an instructor I've not had to break that many hearts. Oh, I've had my share of folks who, when they fail the riding skills evaluation, you breathe a sigh of relief and are happy you can suggest another training go round, but that's not hard.

You may have faced the hard thing as well. Telling someone (or yourself) that, "Yeah, one beer is too many to ride," *or* you may have to tell someone you're scared to ride with them, or you're scared *for* them. Hard things can often be awkward things. Here's some thoughts that will come to mind when you are facing hard things:

"Someone's got to tell them."

"Who else can I ask?"

"CRAP, CRAP, CRAP, CRAP, CRAP!"

Here's one that runs out to center stage of your mind waving and screaming, "LOOK AT ME!" yet also makes a lot sense: "They need to learn this the hard way." It's usually an excuse, *but* it's also true once in a while.

There's a ton of excuses that hop into your mind when your mom asks you to head down to the funeral home and dress your pop, but she's your Mom; someone has to do it, and eventually you have to cowboy up and do the hard thing no matter how much you don't want to. You may not want to tell a friend they're too drunk to ride. You won't look forward to telling a friend you think their riding days are over, but don't you owe it to them to talk it over? When your riding buddy has a spectacularly bad idea, shouldn't you say something?

Yeah, sometimes you just have to cowboy up and do the hard thing.

# AUTHORITY

Ever been pulled over? Come on—admit it. If you ride a bike you've probably been in the warm embrace of a traffic stop. The tight throat, the "I can't catch my breath" moment, the fumbling with gloves and helmet, looking for your ID, registration, proof of insurance...

Remember? I remember one night I got pulled over by the most astonishingly pretty female officer. I was shocked. I had been playing in the back lot at work earlier in the day, and my super sloppy teen-aged hack job of a taillight assembly (about as bright as a candle) was covered in mud and filth, and this lovely officer had pulled me over to see what was up with that. It was about eleven at night, and about two minutes into the stop her backup arrived and BAM! Another female officer— just as pretty as the first. I was eighteen and all these "Dear Penthouse" thoughts were bouncing around in my head...*but* I was smart enough to keep my dang mouth shut. (I worked up a really killer opener too: "Where do they hide you in the daytime?" Which I could follow up with, "You can frisk me if you want to!" Which would lead to: "Now that I'm cuffed and in the car could someone please pick up my teeth?" *or* "Could

I have a drink of water? My testicles are caught in my throat...")

Ahhhhh, youth. It is very important to know what to say and when to say it. As mentioned, I teach high school. It's the Land of the Lost, a place of experimentation and exploration. Kids get to try on different personas and styles. Ideally, they come out complete humans; all grown-up and well mannered. In education we call things like that "social competencies." Social competencies are things like: Tonality; knowing what tone to use—sarcastic, empathetic, firm, *and* being able to distinguish them in others. Volume; how loud should I talk in church? Talking loudly at the funeral is bad. Proximity; are you standing too close? Personal space. The ability to follow instructions, wait in line, or take turns is another social competency.

Ever been somewhere and there's that one person who walks in late, pushes to the front, talks too loud, stands too close, and is just a pain in the butt? Yeah, they're not necessarily self-absorbed narcissists, they may be socially incompetent. They just plain don't know how important it is to obey society's subtle little rules; no one ever taught them to say "please". Let me give you an example:

We've established I work at a high school. I started teaching when I was thirty-eight. Yeah, I'm not a wake up at twelve and walk in to the kitchen, call a family meeting, and announce, "I'm going to be a High School Teacher," sort of guy. I'm a "Hey, you ever think about teaching? Wanna give it a try?" "Sure, why not? Can't be worse than what I'm doing now!" kind of guy. When I walk down the halls at school I don't see fresh, young, excited, eager minds waiting to be filled with literary and historical goodness; I see myself and all my hooligan friends trying to work the seam and grift the system.

If I'm walking down the hall and I see three or four kids standing around during what should be class hours, I walk up and ask, "Where are we supposed to be, Guys?" Why do I do that? Cause the alpha will answer. He or she always does. There's a leader, and the leader will look you in the eyes and try to measure you up. Is this teacher going to bust chops? Can we take him?

Will he fold? Do I tell him a lie? How do I maintain position in my group. The *fun* thing is that the betas will step back. It's amazing when you walk up to a bunch of kids and ask, "Where are we supposed to be, Guys?" The alpha will confront you and the betas will start to physically back away. Why? 'Cause I'm an alpha and I just walked up and now I'm not backing down! And who doesn't like to see an alpha/alpha fight?

Omegas. They're the hangers-on, the last animal in the pack to eat—the frightened ones who probably don't belong and are the first to get slapped. Once I've pinned down the alpha I'll turn to the kid who's backing away the fastest or looks the most worried; that's the omega. I'll address him directly and say: "Where are you supposed to be right now?" Omegas will immediately blurt out, "I'm a TA for Mr. Jones!" or "Restroom break from Ms. Smith." To which I'll say: "Scamper like a bunny, get where you belong." Social competency is a must have for omegas; keeping their heads down, fitting in, not sticking out is vital for their survival. In a situation where there is clearly going to be conflict and danger, the socially competent omega children will understand that I'm giving them a chance to get out of the blast radius, and they'll often start volunteering places they should be right at the very moment, and I'll say: "Scamper," and they'll go right where they're supposed to be. Why? Because an omega kid is a survivor kid, and a survivor kid understands that they got caught and are getting a break. They'll take the break when it's offered. They'll run. If the alpha dies, they'll find another pack, another alpha, another social group. They are classic followers.

You've heard of betas, yes? A beta will hang out to see what happens. Why? Because if the alpha dies—the beta inherits the pack. Betas will also look to follow the alpha's lead. Betas make great wingmen, they'll help the alpha and are happy to be part of the action and *not* an omega. I've been trying to figure out for years if Robin was Batman's beta or an omega. What a great Comic-Con panel debate that would be. Maybe that's why Robin bit the big one, he was an uppity beta looking to go alpha.

Unfortunately, sometimes in some groups it's pretty easy to be the alpha. A weak sauce group may have an alpha who is not socially competent. Example:

I'm walking down the hallway during my prep hour; a peaceful, quiet stroll that I pass off as exercise. It's a placid moment, there shouldn't be any students in the halls unless they have a pass. Eager minds should all be ensconced in books and desks and learning. Yet, as I walk I spot a pair of young men. One small, one big; a real Mutt & Jeff pair. They look...wrong. They don't have the clean cut, well groomed, "won't disturb other's in the library" Teacher's Aide look. Are they clutching passes? No. Are they avoiding eye contact? Yes! To the point—once I make eye contact they don't even attempt to *look* like they're trying to do something. I mean, really, at least turn and start walking, look like you're discussing the 100 Years War and shuffle like you're going somewhere. *Nope.* Just standing there being socially incompetent. I decide to investigate.

"Where are we supposed to be, Gentlemen?" I ask as I roll gently in.

The little one looks up at me and says: "Right here." BOOM! Socially incompetent alpha? Or Beta trying to make his bones? I mean really, come on; who says that to an authority figure unless they're incompetent or looking for negative attention? It's a "Please Sir, would you bust my chops?" I have to respond and, oddly, I have a question ready. Why—'cause it's shocking how often you get the "Right here" answer.

"So your schedule says: second hour, standing around in hallway?" says I.

"Yeah, right here." And then he turns his back on me. Wow.

I look the big one in the eye and ask him, "Where are you supposed to be right now?"

Not even a pause, and he says, "Ms. Hart's room. Biology."

"Come on," I say, "I'll walk you there." Down the hall we go. If you've been in a school built in the last fifteen years you'll find that there's three main building materials: cinder block, sheetrock, and tile. As you walk you'll hear that industrial echo that tile-floored hospitals used to have; with every sound zinging off the floor and bouncing off the walls until (in theory) it's mitigated by the acoustic ceiling tiles. There's a bit of a "green mile" feeling as you walk a kid somewhere; it's tense, it's nervous, it's perfect for some Q&A, a little interrogation.

Looking at the big guy I point to the little one and ask, "He's not in your class is he?"

"No, Sir." Good. I'll shave off the big one and be able to see what's the little one's problem.

Looking back at the little one I ask, "Who's class are you supposed to be in?"

And, I swear this is true, he says, "The tall guy, you know the one with hair."

I stopped walking. They stopped walking. "You're kidding me," I said, "fifteen weeks into a semester and you don't know your teacher's name?"

"He's the tall one," waving his hand over his head with a strange coiffing motion he adds, "with hair."

I was floored. What do you say? "As opposed to the tall one without hair?"

We start walking again. We go upstairs. At Mrs. Hart's room the big kid asks, "Can I go?" I say, "Yes," and he disappears into the biology lab. I turn to the little one and say, "Where are you supposed to be? Where's the tall teacher with hair's room?"

"Down here," he says and we start walking. And keep walking. Our alpha stops and looks in the windows in the doors of all the classrooms. (They're called Hostage Windows if you're interested.) We do two entire laps of the upstairs of the building. I stop.

"What's going on?" I ask.

"Can't see anyone I know," he says. It's important to know at this point in the story that the district I work for has an A/B schedule. This means that each student has only four classes a day but each class is 87 minutes long. For guys like me who teach professional technical courses this is great because you can

get the gear out, get to work and have 60 or 70 minutes to get
something done before you have to start clean up.

"Come on." I look him in the eye. "Let's go to the attendance
office and see where you're supposed to be." Different levels of
social competence exhibit different behaviors, and this kid's not
entirely incompetent; he understands the basic concept that he's
in my custody, he's pliant, his tone is correct, he is polite, good
volume, he's...meek. It's a good sign. Maybe he was just having
a bad day, and his mouthing off was an attempt at some kind of
lashing at authority.

Arriving at the Attendance Office I ask the secretary to
look up our boy's schedule so I can return him to wherever it
is he should be. It turns out he's supposed to be in the portable
classrooms that are in the back lot while they finish the new high
school.

Shocked, he looks up and says, "Today's an A day?"

And a Tuesday to boot. Which means our boy wasn't at
school Monday. It's just that obvious. Often with an A/B day
schedule students arrive Monday not knowing if it's an A or a B
day. They've been gone two days. They had dates. Some stayed at
Dad's house, some stayed at Mom's, it's a tough time to be a kid
and sometimes on a Monday, they forget where they are on the
schedule.

But they *always* know what day Tuesday is. Monday is an
A day?—Tuesday is a B. Monday is a B day?—Tuesday is an A.
They don't forget what yesterday was; which means our boy here
*wasn't at school* yesterday.

"Hold up," I pause and stare this kid right in the eye and ask,
"What's his attendance look like?"

The secretary punches a couple of keys and says: "21 unverified
absences," and adds, "he needs to see the Dean of Students." Boom.
Hammer. Thunder. Insert body slam, pile driver, coyote meets
brick wall metaphor/sound/image. Ow. Hear the swooooosh of
the flush? All because he had to say: "Right here."

Design is a tricky business. You need to have related offices
close together and the Dean of Students office is about twelve

feet from the Attendance Secretary's desk, and all she does is look and see that there's no students in the Boss's office, then calls out, "Do you have a moment?" Then the disembodied voice of the eavesdropping Dean returns, "Sure, send him in."

All this is too delicious or tragic or poetic to miss. "I'll take him in," I volunteer. "Come on," I say, and we take the short walk to the Dean of Students. Five steps later we're in front of the Dean of Students.

One phone call and the whole story is out. Expelled from another school district, our hero is a "sleep in," a student that is living with a relative (sister) so he can attend ours. His sister and her husband work; so everyday our boy goes home, collects the mail (removing any notices from the school), checks the answering machine (deleting all messages from the school), and then does whatever the heck he pleases. It's the life of Riley. No homework. Get up *after* your sis and brother-in-law are gone, watch Sports Center, drop by the school for lunch, hang out with some of your buds as you all cut class—you know the sort of stuff *we* used to try to do.

Until our parents found out. Like his did. On the phone. It was a crushing moment. His life was changing forever. A check of his grade showed all Fs. After the call I turned to excuse myself, and I asked him a question: "How could you have avoided all this?"

"I don't know," was his answer. Truly innocent. This, I realize is a teaching moment. We can equip this kid with something he can use for the rest of his life.

"Let me tell you something." I start, "You could have avoided this by busting your chops, doing the homework, gritting your teeth, and doing your job—which is to be a student. That's what a teacher should tell you." I lean in, "But I'll tell you a secret; I'm not a teacher by calling. I didn't wake up one day in high school and say 'I want to be a teacher!' I'm a working guy who teaches kids how to work.

"Here's where you went wrong. I asked you where you were supposed to be, and you said 'Right here.' If you had been able to tell me where you were supposed to be and started walking that way—I would have let you go.

"Here's something for you to think about. When you get pulled over by a cop, and he comes up to the window and asks: 'Do you know why I pulled you over?'

"Don't answer: 'Cause you're a dick.' Because if you do, you'll end up spread-eagled on the asphalt with a cop kneeling on your head."

With that I took my metaphorical knee off his head and left him with the patrol sergeant.

What does this have to do with riding? Simple: If a cop pulls you over and asks: "Do you know why I pulled you over?"

Don't say, "Cause you're a dick." Maybe modulate your tone, watch your volume, choose your words carefully. Be respectful, be courteous, and don't poke the bear. Odds are you don't want a full cavity search.

# PERSONAL SAFETY

Ever had another driver get really angry with you? It happens occasionally you know. There was a story that ran in our local paper not too long ago about a young lady in a pickup truck who, after cutting off a guy in a sedan, chased him. She threw coins and little packets of ranch dressing at his car. Eventually, she followed him off the freeway, into a parking lot and then rammed his car three times. Yeah, I read somewhere that women are more likely to use a car as a weapon in road rage situations. (It makes sense; guys want to punch it out in the street). The police were summoned and the young lady arrested.

Now, remember she rammed his car three times in a parking lot; which means she went off the freeway and into the community. Meaning she followed him. She chased him. She pursued him. Imagine if her victim had been on a motorcycle instead of in a car. Every so often you'll hear stories about road rage that document instances of drivers acting with malice toward bikers. Heck, you may even have been on the receiving end of some unwelcome automobile attention. Remember, this *is* America, and you don't have to be a rocket scientist, or even overly lucid, to get a license to drive or ride. With that in mind I thought I'd take a moment to share some basic security tips that people in television use to keep anchors, reporters, photographers, and other personnel safe. I'm going to apply them to motorcycles and show you some of the risks and rewards of being aware of your surroundings and having an escape plan.

1. Avoid having a predictable pattern. Have at least three different routes between your work and home. Alternate routes randomly. If someone is mad at you and knows you'll be on your bike at a specific time in a specific place—you're at risk. If you have an incident on the way to work or home, alter your route for the next few days, this gives the other driver time to cool off and forget you. If a driver feels you cut them off at an intersection, feels slighted enough to honk or flip you off, and then sees you the next day, you can become a target of opportunity. It's best to avoid them for a day or two, so use an alternate route. Varying your time of departure and arrival can help you avoid the scene of an "incident."

2. If you think you're being followed "Walk the Box." Make four consecutive right-hand turns. Go around the block. It may be a *big* block but there is *no reason on earth* for someone to make four rights turns behind you, unless they are following you. If they do, then they *are* following you. You are now a potential target. Behave accordingly (see #3).

3. Once you fear, or know, you're being followed, proceed to a well lit, well populated area. This sounds awful, but place yourself where there are witnesses. Witnesses will help confirm your account of what happens and often serve as good Samaritans. Knowing where the local police station, substation, or barracks are located is a good thing too. Go to the police station parking lot and pull right up to the door. If you're being followed—they'll peel off. *If* they follow you into the parking lot, just park it by the door and lay on the horn. Officers will respond. (Come on, there's a bike up on the sidewalk by the front door laying on the horn! They'll come out.) Police Stations tend to be populated 24/7 but be aware that at two in the morning in small municipalities you might not have an officer on duty at the station.

4. Keep a log of vehicles you are having trouble with. *If* every few days that orange Mazda is giving you the finger, take note of the model, year, and plate number. Once you're at work or home write up a description of the driver and a short note of what they're doing. This may sound nuts but you'll have documentation if something happens. (*And* you'll realize that you need to vary your route to avoid problems.)

You don't need to be a target. *If* you're having a problem the best way to behave is classic motorcycle safety—don't place yourself in a bad position. *Avoid* places where you're having problems. One place that can make you feel particularly exposed is freeway riding. Let's face it, if you're being harassed on the freeway you can feel pretty exposed—where can you turn off? Where can you run? A couple of thoughts on how to handle road rage incidents on the freeway:

1. You're better off getting them in front of you if you can. One of the problems with being pursued is that you have to watch in front as well as behind. *If* you can get them alongside and the situation is clear enough, you can out-brake them. What if they stop? Well, then you stop. If they get out of the car? Use acceleration to your advantage.

2. Exit the freeway *into* an urban or suburban area. This puts you in a lower speed environment that plays to your strengths, so exiting is a good idea. (As you demonstrated).

3. Even on the freeway there are other users you can use to block a pursuing car. You'll fit in smaller spaces and can hopefully evade a following car. *Hopefully* other users will recognize you're being pursued and may call law enforcement for help.

4. Although it's tempting, *speeding up* probably only makes things worse. With speed come all the problems with handling, braking, time/distance, and traffic. If you speed up then you're moving forward through traffic, yes? Of course—which means you're coming up to and passing cars that might not expect you. If they don't expect you and make a sudden move into your path then all that speed that was working for you is now working against you! You trade the danger of an irrational person for the danger of inattentive people. Worse yet, that knucklehead behind

you might not have given up the chase and now you're working a path through potentially preoccupied drivers while trying to keep one eye in the mirror. Best to get off the freeway and into a better environment, one suited to your evasion strengths.

IF you are pursued remember that you're dealing with an irrational human being! They are pursuing you because they are, realistically, OUT OF CONTROL. They are unpredictable and dangerous—IF you do lose them on the freeway you might consider stopping at a call box or pulling over and using a cell phone to REPORT the incident so you can have a record of what happened. As always, once you're out of harm's way I would suggest exiting the freeway IMMEDIATELY and altering your route so you don't find that car waiting for you three miles up.

As always, noting time of day, type of vehicle, license info, driver description will help in case you run into that same car again next week...

A couple of final thoughts; first, cars are big! They weigh a couple of tons. As a weapon they are profoundly dangerous to motorcyclists and you want to avoid confrontations with them. What's the old saying? "Don't bring a knife to a gunfight"? A car's strength as a weapon are size, weight and low risk of operator injury. A driver running over a rider is at very little risk. YOU, the rider, are extremely vulnerable. Use your head to stay out of bad situations. Don't escalate them. FLEE. You can split lanes, ride up on the sidewalk, out brake, out turn and out accelerate most automobiles. Use this to your advantage. If you need to flee, turn into that parking lot, double back, slip between stopped cars, evade—don't fight.

Yeah, fleeing isn't as glamorous as fighting, but you can't beat up an SUV with your gloved fists when a driver decides to park it on you. Even if it's a crime, you're still the one doing the hospital tme. As much as those armored gloves and that DOT approved helmet give you a sense of invincibility, they won't do you any good against a pickup that has decided to run you down.

# EVERY PART IS IMPORTANT

Like high schools everywhere, the one I work at has a student parking lot and a faculty parking lot. On weekends at the school we teach Idaho STAR motorcycle training. It's a state-run program (one of the best in the country), and I'm an instructor with the program. It's not like I'm biased, it's really a good program. But I digress.

On weekends when I have a motorcycle teaching gig, I arrive early, about seven am, cone-off the range, and do a quick walk FOD check of the range. FOD is a military term meaning "foreign object debris"—basically it's crap that shouldn't be on the tarmac that can get sucked up into an engine and disable a plane. At a high school you find some curious FOD; things like: pop bottles and cans, pom-poms, sandwiches, water bottles, a bound copy of Mary Shelly's Frankenstein, a not so bound copy of the US history book the juniors use, condoms (sealed and open), several cans of whipped cream, and lots of nuts and bolts.

Yeah, nuts and bolts. You'll be walking around just giving it the FOD walk and you'll find bolts that look like engine mounts, nuts that look like lug nuts, large and small you'll find them all, even the occasional spark plug or gas cap. It's truly an odd assortment of bits and pieces.

I'm in the habit of picking up said nut or bolt and asking the other instructor, "Do you think this looks important?" Or "Figure somebody's missing this right now?" Why? Because I think it's funny that someone's running around with a part flapping in the breeze. Is that so wrong? Hey, I'm evil, I teach high school—what did you expect? Besides I've also been the guy who looks under the hood to see what that weird sound is only to realize I didn't torque the alternator down. (Battery won't hold a charge? MAYBE IT'S NOT GETTING ONE! Grrr...)

Every part is important. Remember the "for want of a nail the shoe was lost, for want of a shoe the horse was lost, for want of a horse the rider was lost, for want of a rider the battle was lost...blah blah blah" story? Well, it's actually a pretty good story. Every part *is* important. Imagine landing a plane without lug nuts or cooking with a skillet that didn't have a handle. How about riding a motorcycle without a foot peg? Yeah, that's tough. Seen it twice. First time a friend of mine fell over on a tricky mountain road and when we got up the pin that holds the foot peg on had sheared. He could hook his heel on the nubs sticking off the frame and then ride home. Using the rear brake was close to impossible, but he managed to get home safely.

The second time was a couple of weekends ago. I had snuck into an Experienced Course and was doing the riding segment of the day. I was a "student rider," and we were working in a big school parking lot. I had decided to ride because a friend of mine was in the course, and I thought it would be fun. Which it was. Until he fell over doing a low speed turn and snapped off the mounting bracket that held his foot peg. Low speed fall, maybe three miles-per-hour, right side, snapped it at the frame; the only thing holding the bracket to the bike was the hydraulic brake line.

Now, if you're a not a motorcyclist and you're reading this, the best analogy I can give you is: imagine riding a bicycle with kickback brakes that is missing a pedal. *That's* what I'm talking about. Your balance is screwed up, you can't put weight on one side, and you can't brake well.

It's really a mess.

Every part is important—and they're important all the time. "But Crash," you ask sweetly, "brakes aren't important when you're accelerating!" *Contraire mon frer!* What if your brakes are dragging, not fully released? That could profoundly affect acceleration. *Plus* what if your acceleration puts you in desperate need of your brakes? "I was gonna slow down officer, but my brakes are really bad..." *and* you prefer the low thread counts of hospital sheets. You never know when a part is going to be important. How 'bout your brake lines, or oil drain plug, or piston rings, or under or over-torqued head bolts, throttle cable, triple clamp, or seat? (Ever ride a bike without a seat? It's not as fun as it sounds. Don't ask.)

Every part is important all the time because you never know when you may need them and if they become a mission-critical part and they aren't in good repair—the mission can fail, spectacularly. *Or* you may get lucky and slide by without it for a time only to find out when you really needed it the part wasn't ready for the load.

Take hockey as an example—when the puck is on the other side of the rink the goalie doesn't have much to do. Watch and you'll see them sneak a drink from the water bottle they keep in the top of the net; however, you'll never see them leave the ice! And when they're sneaking that drink they *never* take their eyes off the puck. They may not be an active part of the play, but they keep their head in the game.

Where's the big "Life" tie in? I got yer big "Life" metaphor right here:

Everybody is important. You may feel like the bolt holding a fender on. You may think "this isn't a glamorous gig like a piston or the fuel tank"—and you're right it's not flashy and exciting but it *is* important. Fenders protect us from road debris, water, and anything that can be flung up from the tires. Ever ride a bike without a fender? Crap goes everywhere and it's decidedly dangerous in mud or rain; your vision is impaired, crap hits you in the face...

Feeling more like a hand grip? Not as sexy as a cool pair of drag bars, but we need those bad boys. They cushion shock, provide grip, improve comfort, dampen vibes. Sometime when you're changing grips, cut the old ones off and ride without them for a second—shockingly bad.

Lawyer, doctor, mechanic...physicist, publicist, police...fry cook, firefighter, Flamenco dancer—whatever it is you do you're also friend, mentor, companion, brother, sister, father, son, mother, daughter; we're all part of a family either by blood or spirit. We're all linked to each other, and the things we do make everyone's life better. Don't buy into the idea that you're not important. Just a simple act of compassion in the grocery store can turn someone's day around and, in turn, they pass that along and pretty soon things are a whole lot better for all of us. We all affect all the parts we're connected to.

Now get out there and be the be the best damn side stand you can be.

(See, you didn't realize it but you're actually holding the whole thing up!)

# IS CRASHING INEVITABLE?

You've heard it: "There are two kinds of motorcyclists, those that have crashed, and those that will crash". Is it true? Is crashing inevitable? Does every single motorcyclist have a fated destiny on the deck? Are we doomed to fall? I think it's a valuable question. Do we all crash? Should we accept it as a rite of passage? Or is this "you will crash" thing the hobgoblin of a lazy mind?

I've crashed—hence the name "Captain Crash". One particularly spectacular recreational hill climbing disaster at Hollister cemented that title. But...maybe every dirt biker *does* crash! On a dirt bike it's part of the territory; but what about street riding? Does every street rider crash? I have. Twice. In 1982. Both were my fault. One was the result of grabbing a big hand full of brakes while swerving, the other was poor traction management in a freshly "sealed" road; both were my fault. Trained by friends, I, shall we say, learned by hard knocks not to brake while swerving *and* not to chop the throttle when the rear steps out.

Both were avoidable drops. Both happened under 30 mph, classic Hurt Study stuff—managed a little evasive/corrective action, hit the ground about 20mph. Bottom line? Super normal street fall; nothing special, no injuries, no major damage, no

175

police reports. Although one guy did stop after one, asked if I was OK, said he had seen the whole thing if I needed a witness, gave me his business card (Chiropractor) and told me to call if I needed anything.

My crashes were *avoidable*. Probably with training I would have had a better skill set. I would have been warned to enter a turn with sketchy traction slower or would have known what a space cushion was and not have been tailgating. I'd have *known* that there were risks, and I could have managed them better.

I'm not going to argue that everybody tips over. You drop your bike in the garage. You might put your foot on oil at the gas pump and have one of those groin pulling, slapstick, Three Stooges-style slides to the ground. A U-turn in the parking lot may turn into a faceplant. It happens. You catch your boot on the turn signal getting on. Crap happens; *but* we are not *all* going to crash. There is a good chance we might. But fortune isn't cast. We can do things to avoid it.

First—Don't accept failure. With "everybody crashes" comes an implicit excuse for poor riding. Buying into "everybody crashes" means you've mentally quit. You *have*. It's gonna happen, right? So when that semi turns in front of you, your mindset isn't "act—save yourself" your mindset is suddenly "well, here's that crash I knew was coming." Syracuse doesn't get beat by a team that expects to lose. The number-six seed beats the number-one seed when the number-six seed *believes* they can win.

Axiom: Don't quit before the game starts. Imagine if you were an athlete and the coach came in pregame and said, "Everybody loses. *Everybody*. Now, let's get out there!"

Second—Understand that we might fail. As soon as you say, "Can't happen to me," you've placed yourself securely in the arms of danger; you've surrendered your vigilance. When you refuse to turn and face danger, it jumps on your back an slits your throat— often. Turning to look at danger often drives it off.

Axiom: The first defense to danger is recognizing it's there. Risk unseen or ignored is risk unmanaged. Risk unmanaged is... just dumb.

Third—Control your destiny. If you want to learn to ride, *get trained.* Don't accept a crappy teacher—and Bunkie, *you* are a crappy teacher. Self-teaching and discovery-learning do work. Bump your head and you'll learn to duck—but why bang your head? Learn from the mistakes of others. Most, if not all curriculum, is based on research, and that research asks a basic question: "What happened, why did it happen, and what can future riders do to avoid it happening to them?" Riders get up off the ground, and they ask the same question: "What happened?" Then they go out and work not to make the same mistake again.

Axiom: *Everybody* knows more than *just you.* Find the pools of common truths. Learn from the mistakes of others. Take a course. Find knowledge and embrace it. Train, read, talk, practice. You don't need to crash to learn how not to.

Not everybody crashes. Not everybody drops their bike in the garage. You might; but then again you might not. The first step to *not* falling is accepting that you *might* and then working like hell not to.

# WHERE

Can you imagine saying: "There are two kinds of people, those that have cancer and those that will"? Yet the sentiment that every biker *will* fall is common.

As soon as you say *everybody* does, I'll go to the bar and find a one-eyed, grizzled outlaw rider who never wears a helmet and has *never* crashed! Yes, you'll find them. The first thing we need to do is define what is a "crash."

Is a slow tip over in the parking lot during a U-turn a crash?

When you ride up next to your buddies, stop, and just tip over—a crash?

You're getting off your bike in the garage and your boot hooks your grab rail and you pull the bike down—is that a crash?

In Crash World (a fully owned subsidiary of Capt. Crash life) the bike falls over; lots of bikes fall over. In fact, a majority of bikes fall over at some point. However falling over and a crash are *not* the same things.

A crash is something that starts at speed, and results in rider and bike both on the ground. It spits you off. You wind up skittering down the pavement. See, we call a bike falling over "a crash" to make it sound more dramatic than it is. It isn't as stupid and embarrassing to have "crashed" in a parking lot as it is to "forget to put the kickstand down and couldn't hold the bike up."

I'm always offended when someone equates falling over with a crash. To equate having a car turn into your path of travel at 35 mph and then striking that car with slipping in diesel at the gas station is just wrong. They're two entirely different things. One, the car, was the most common accident that happens to motorcyclists. The other is just the inability or unwillingness or carelessness of not looking where you're gonna put your feet.

You go up your favorite road, get to speed, get surprised by sand, lose the front, and wind up sliding 300 ft.—you *crashed.*

Drop your bike in the parking lot?—*Not* a crash.

And yes, I have crashed. And they didn't have to happen, and they were my fault. The last one was in a middle school parking lot, going about 30-35 mph. I actually knew there was a high likelihood of a crash. I was pushing it, and I knew I was. I also knew in the grand scheme of things that it wasn't a place where things, if they went wrong, would result in a helicopter ride.

See, that's the *where* part. *Where* are you doing the things that might result in a crash?

A crash generally is caused by one of three things:

1. Going to the edge of the envelope *in the wrong place.* Yup, this won't be popular, but sand trucks never spill on the *track.* Deer don't jump out on the *track.* Minivans aren't on the *track* with you. Diesel isn't drooling out of the VW Rabbit on the *track.* If you're going to the edge of the envelope, then you should do it in an appropriate place. I would add doing wheelies in the middle of a pack of touring sportbikes is probably the wrong place—if you're stunting, go stunt; if you're road racing, go road racing. Bottom line is *where* you do things can multiply the risks exponentially. Going down at 90 on a track is entirely different than doing it on the top of the canyon.

2. Painfully bad luck—generally exacerbated by doing the wrong thing in the wrong place. Yeah, you're pushing the edge of the envelope on the Lowman Road and *bad luck* strikes, and you end up running through a big puddle of anti-freeze you can't avoid because you're carrying too much speed. If you hadn't been riding too fast *where* you were, you'd have had a chance. *But* even at cautious, legal speeds you still might have had a problem.

3. Others' poor decisions. Number one wreck? Used to be someone left-turns in front of you, and you hit them; rumor is that's changed. I don't know; I do know that sometimes you just get reamed. Bad things happen, others make bad decisions, and we sometimes have to pay for them. Call it fate.

So what does it all mean? Well, we all had that crazy aunt who said, "Everyone who rides a motorcycle dies." *She was wrong.* Buying into her nutty cousin's idea that, "There are two kinds of bikers, those that have crashed and those that will," is *crap.* If you believe that, just take a sledgehammer to your bike now—it's gonna get mangled anyway, right?

You don't *have* to get heart disease. You don't *have* to get cancer. You don't *have* to have a stroke. You can eat right, you can exercise, you can manage your risk factors—and you may do everything right and *still* get heart disease, cancer, or have a stroke. All you can do is manage the things you have control over.

Not everybody crashes. *Tons* of us fall over. Some of us crash—do not buy into the wrong-headed idea that everyone does. If everyone who rode a motorcycle crashed and died, then there'd be a much bigger used-bike market, you couldn't get insurance, and the government would be outlawing single track vehicles.

It's not *when*—it's *if,* and most importantly *where.* Where do you put yourself into the risk zone? Where are you engaging in high-risk behaviors that increase your chances of crashing? Are you aware of your surroundings when you ride? Are you living a little farther in the future when you're in traffic?

It's on you, not fate. You don't *have to* crash. Control your situation, manage your risk, be aware of your surroundings—and yes, you might crash, but at least you did everything you could to avoid it.

# "Missing the Dan"

Looking ahead while riding a motorcycle is a basic skill every motorcyclist should have and practice. It is not an advanced skill, it is a basic skill. However, like many things your fundamentals can be messed up and you can still survive. It's true, but it will catch up to you eventually.

You really want to see someone with flawed fundamentals get beat up? Watch "Hell's Kitchen" where they bring in working, moderately successful chefs and as the show goes on things get tricky and their flawed fundamental skills are exposed, and they eventually fail—sometimes spectacularly.

They can cook. They just aren't chefs. Make sense?

Looking where you want to go is a lot like being on "Hell's Kitchen." If things are simple, a lack of a basic skill can be covered. You can "fake it 'til you make it." Missing fundamentals can be covered up, strengths will hide weaknesses, and, well, you can fudge it your whole riding career and get away with it, if you're lucky.

You may know I'm not a proponent of the "every motorcyclist crashes" theory. I don't buy it because *not* every motorcyclist crashes. The difference, other than bad luck, is when a rider gets themselves into a situation that exposes a fundamental flaw in their skill set. Suddenly a situation requires sound fundamentals, and lacking them, the rider crashes.

Looking well ahead—looking where you want to go—is one of those skills that when you need it and you don't have it, it will leave you on the ground cussing.

Let me share the situation that showed me that visual leading was a fundamental skill. I was riding from Idaho City to Lowman with two friends, one on a Kawasaki ZRX1100 and one on a Kawasaki ZX-9R. I was riding my old Suzuki GSXR-1100 (last of the oil cooled ones).

This is a classic mountain road, one lane each way, lots of double yellow, occasional turnouts for slow moving vehicles, short visual leads—you know, the stuff we live for!

We climbed up out of Idaho City, rode over the Moore's Creek Summit, and turning down toward Lowman we cut it loose. Yes, it's tight up there, but it's also fun and there's those straights for passing.

My pal on the ZX-9 had dropped back, a wise call, and Dan and I were hustling pretty good, just zipping along. Just before Beaver Creek (I believe is the name) as you travel to Lowman you make a tight, slightly off-camber right, hit a little chicane, and then make a 180 degree left, and switch into the old Lowman Fire Burn. There is a two to three hundred foot drop there and no guard rail.

Dan was exiting the turn a little wide, his front caught the paint stripe, and he tucked it. BANG! He was on the ground.

As with most terrifying situations, time slowed down for me. I remember getting on the brakes, and the bike straightening up. I know this sounds dumb, but the first thought in my head was, "Dang, the bottom of Dan's bike is really dirty," followed by "look at all the pretty sparks!"

As the bike slid and spun away, I looked at Dan who was

rolling and sliding on the pavement. Trust me, having done the slide and roll thing, it is very interesting to see from the other side. The only thought in my head became, "Don't hit Dan; DON'T HIT DAN; DON'T HIT DAN!" and I looked directly into his eyes. I made eye contact, and I thought, "I'm gonna spear DAN!"

Then a little voice in my head said, "Where do you want to go?" and I looked over to my right and down the road where I wanted to be. That picture, of the road I wanted to take, is *burned* into my mind to this day.

I turned my head, looked, and went.

Dan's bike and Dan slid to a stop about three feet from going over the edge.

In looking at tire marks on the road and in the dirt, it was clear I had been skidding the rear in a straight line toward the edge, had released the rear, which left the pavement, carved an arc with it in the two-foot-wide space between the pavement and drop off, and then crossed back over into my own lane to make a controlled, safe stop.

Basically, I had slewed the back out, flat-tracked the back off the pavement, kept the front hooked up, and changed directions, then continued on to stop safely.

I have no idea how. All I can see are two competing visions: one of looking Dan right in the eye and expecting to hit him and one of that ribbon of asphalt where I *wanted* to be and where I *went* when I looked at it.

Now, if all that was required to ride a motorcycle was looking, which would be followed by going, then we would all look and then go! I believe my years as a dirt biker probably were what got that big Gixxer turned because—looking at it today—I'm sure that the back tracked out and I spun it up to get it turned once I was out of shape and had the front end on the pavement and the back in the dirt. (A dirt bike fundamental is steering with the rear end and I believe that is what I did). But, all the dirt bike fundamentals were useless until I looked where I wanted to go.

Keep your head and eyes up. Look where you want to go. Look at the Dan—Hit the Dan. Look to your escape route. Look to safety—Go to safety.

It's not easy, but you *can* do it.

# Assuming

One of the dangers that riders face is getting caught up in riding *fast* on the street. I've ridden pretty quick on the street. Defining the dangers of "robust" street riding is difficult, so I won't try. I just want to attack one issue: the ten foot path. What is the ten foot path? American roads tend to be about twenty feet wide, ten feet per lane. (There's actually federal guidelines on truck traffic and how wide lanes need to be according to how much traffic they get).

Those ten foot lanes create a very interesting mirage for riders: the idea that our path of travel is twenty feet wide. Riders look at the *whole* road and it works a magic in their head that makes them think, "Look at all that space," and they assume that all that elbow room is theirs for the taking. Which is true *and* false. Sure, the road is twenty feet wide but *your* lane is only ten. Once you cross that yellow line in the middle, you're in someone else's path. You're over the border, in enemy territory, you've got no rights. You're the guy standing in a stranger's kitchen at midnight—shooting you is OK. Yes, the ten feet on the right are yours but that's it. Another thought; if you're within eighteen inches of the center line, you're starting to poke your handlebar out into the opposing lane.

Let's do the math; ten feet minus eighteen inches is eight and a half feet. Taking into consideration that as you approach the outside of the lane you have the symmetrical issue of sticking your handlebar out over the fog line and into the shrubbery... you have...18 + 18 = 36, thirty-six inches is three feet, ten foot lane minus three feet is...seven feet. You've got a guarantee of a path of travel that is seven feet wide. (Stupid math. Damn you, Algebra! You with your cold calculations! I've got your unknown factor right here!)

You do not have twenty feet. You do not have even ten feet. You've got just seven feet or, if it makes you feel better, 84 inches. That's what? Less than Shaq? Yet, on a good mountain twisty a rider (myself still included) will look at that undulating, writhing strip of asphalt and think, "Look at all that room." I am not immune. I go up the local super twisty and start using all the road. I put the wheels up against the center line. I get up and ride the crown trying to get some positive banking out of left-handers. My bars are sticking out into the other lane (as is my melon occasionally). Yes, I can be an idiot when I don't put my mind to it. I'm trying to be better about it but...well, it's a turn dang it! And it's soooo much fun.

See? Anybody can get sucked in.

Thinking you have more room to maneuver than you really do isn't just limited to motorcycling. At my high school, kids often think they have options that don't really exist—like crashing and burning your freshman and sophomore years and expecting to be able to avoid summer school. No, really! A kid will just figure, "I'll take it again next year." It turns out that in our school, you don't get to "just take it next year"; you need to take it in summer school. All those freshman classes? *They're for freshman.* We don't need to hire an extra teacher to teach you what you should have learned last year; we have a program for that, it's called summer school.

Like a car in the opposing lane you were looking to use on your favorite road, it's pretty shocking to find out you're gonna spend the halcyon days of summer in Algebra. (Damn you, Algebra! You vex me!) A fifteen year old kid *assumes* that the extra space of "taking it again next year" is gonna be there. Oddly, when they cross that center line assuming that there's not going to be oncoming traffic, they find that there's a truckload of high stake exit tests, budgets that don't want to pay for an extra teacher to re-teach students, and public anger about student underachievement that's about to smack them in the face.

Once you've deluded yourself into believing you've got a safety buffer that isn't there, a cold shot of reality can be rather bracing. Ever get wide on the exit of a turn and find someone right there in your face? Simply going a little wide and getting crowded by another user in close proximity can put a serious case of the shakes into you. Why? Because you never really thought about how it *could* happen. Like a teenager who decides *not* to read Hamlet in that Senior English class you never realized that, yes, there is a consequence here. "Assuming makes an ass out of u and me" is a truism. Part of the issue here is having a dead cold realism about what you're doing and the consequences thereof. My more dignified father would have said something like, "Don't take anything for granted." In other words, don't figure just because you don't *want* a problem to arise doesn't mean that there won't *be* one. You can't hope your way out of a bind.

Whether your fifteen or fifty, reading the classics or riding the canyons, you need to be aware of your surroundings; you need to be able to place yourself in the *context* of what you're doing. Context is a tricky business; it means understanding the small things and how they fit into the larger picture. You can't look at a twenty foot wide road and assume you own it all, you have to understand that contextually you've got about eight feet to work with. If you take for granted that you can use all twenty feet you'll find that when you get to the final and haven't read Hamlet, you're in a real bind. At the very least you should take a look at the Cliff Notes so you've got a vague idea of what's going on; Ophelia shouldn't be a surprise to you. As a rider? Wear your helmet, wear your gear, remember you're on public roads; *narrow* public roads—act accordingly.

# VISION

When I was eighteen I learned to drive a semi. It was fun. It was a White Freightliner cab-over with a sleeper, a 27 foot front trailer and a 23 foot rear trailer. Richard, who was teaching me to drive, had an Australian Shepherd that rode with him everywhere. We'd be out driving, and that dog would get up on the doghouse (engine cover between the seats) and bark at me when Richard would holler at me. It could be unsettling.

The first thing he taught me was, "Look at least a quarter to a half mile ahead." The idea being that it took so long to stop a fully loaded semi that you needed to live in the future a little bit more than when you're in a car; if you're looking a half mile ahead then you'll have time to slow and evade problems. There aren't as many surprises if you're looking into the future a little.

I remember once, on the 101, when we were hauling bricks and I let my vision slip back down to forty feet. I was just watching the license plate in front of me when Richard said, "Get off the gas," in a very stern voice. Casey's head popped up (Casey was the dog's name if memory serves). "SLOW DOWN, NOW!" he hollered at me. I got off the gas, Casey started barking, suddenly the car forty feet in front of me was on the brakes hard, I was on the brakes hard, and I could FEEEEEEL 80,000lbs of truck and brick pushing hard on my back.

You want to know a sure sign you're in trouble? It's when your "instructor" grabs his dog and puts both feet on the dashboard. That's a bad sign. Remember that. When the guy who knows his craft assumes the crash position, things aren't good.

By now I looked up, saw an opening on the right, and snapped the wheel to the right. Ever play "crack the whip" as a kid? The physics are the same. I cracked the whip. The last axle on the rear trailer actually went up on one wheel. I know cause once things started to be "all-go-to-hell" I looked in the mirror.

Surprisingly, I got stopped with everything intact. The load stayed put. I didn't hit anything. Casey's lungs got a workout. Richard actually told me what went wrong and even had me finish the run.

Fast forward twenty years and I'm riding with a buddy in rush hour traffic. A state trooper has a car pulled over on the left side of the freeway. Since I'm looking well ahead, I see him and all the lookieloos starting to slow down to look, so I roll off the throttle. My buddy rolls off the throttle. The full-sized Dodge pickup in front of us keeps his speed. He's watching the Dodge Neon in front of him. Suddenly the Neon realized the pickup in front of her is no longer moving. She leans hard on the brakes trying to get stopped and does. The pickup behind her suddenly realizes things aren't going well—aren't going at *all* in front of him.

Suddenly I'm looking at blue smoke coming off the pickup in front of me. I slide left and watch as he rear-ends the Neon and impales it on the trailer hitch of the truck in front of it. The cop looks up from his ticket book and sees the whole thing.

I come to a controlled stop, my buddy stops next to me, and I ask, "Should we stay and give a statement?"

"Statement?" He says.

"Witness statement." I say.

"Witness to what?" He says.

He hadn't seen it. He was watching my taillight. I made a

normal, controlled stop and that's all he saw. I told him what happened and he looked around and was shocked. I was living ten seconds further in the future than my buddy, just like Richard had been living ten seconds further in the future with me on the 101.

Keeping your head and eyes up and looking where you're going will give you a real edge on your bike. It buys you precious time to *act*—not *react*—before a situation becomes critical. Sure, there are situations you where you have to react, but what you really want to do is keep yourself in that zone where you don't have to use your emergency skills.

In a few weeks I'll have two kids in college. When they were little kids we started talking about it. What's it take to get there? When do you need to take your SATs? Won't it be cool to be living on your own? Just the pathway issues. Where are we going? Are you looking there? Do you see obstacles in your path? How can you avoid them? How can I get there from here?

You go where you look. Fortunately for me, my first two have caught the vision. My oldest, a girl, didn't even return from her freshman year. She just looked ahead, found a full time job on campus, moved off campus, and now has her own life. My second is going all the way from Idaho to Virginia for college. He wants to be a coach. "Dad, if I want to coach, I need to play college ball. I have to go where that can happen." He's off in a few weeks to report to camp. Sure, it's NAIA football, but like he says, "That sets me apart from the other guys who quit after high school, and with hard work and luck I might transfer and bump up to D1 or D2." He can see where he wants to go and is putting himself on a path to get there.

Motorcycles and the need to look ahead are one of the greatest metaphors you can find. You can apply the things you learn on a motorcycle to lots of life's little situations. Gonna start a business? Where are you trying to go? What is your goal? Buying a car? What do you want it to do? Painting the house? What's the resale value of a pink house in five years?

Head and eyes up, Baby, head and eyes up, look where you want to go. Live a little farther in the future, it'll calm you down and make your life easier. You'll be a safer rider, and you'll get where you want to go.

Honest, it really works.

# Peripheral Vision

Here's an odd thing: when you ride a motorcycle you need to be able to see things you're not looking at. No, really! You do. Oddly enough as you read this you're putting your foveal vision to work. You're looking directly at the word you're reading. Try this—I'll put a word right in the center of the page and then a word at each side. Try to stare at the center word and *read* the words on the side:

RIGHT                    CENTER                    LEFT

Can't look at all three at once? Yep. You're normal. Your "center of gaze" or "center of vision," that part of your eye that is packed with cones and rods and gathers all the hard, fine little details, the "fovea," is really quite small. Almost tiny if you really pay attention to it. Wild. You can *see* the words but reading them is really tough. *Hey!* Let's try it again! Look to the left and see if you can read the center:

Ducati                    Victory                    Honda

Brutal. Here's the deal, you can *see* the words because they are in near your center of vision, but you can't read them because they are actually in your peripheral vision. In fact, your peripheral vision is designed to protect you from danger—like predators and falling trees. Peripheral vision is excellent for sensing *motion*. Try this: Hold your hands out about 45 degrees off center from your body; like you're waiting for a great big hug. Stare straight ahead. You'll be able to see your hands in your peripheral vision. Now, wiggle your fingers. WHAM! See them? That motion is what your peripheral is gonzo great at sensing. (Didn't try it? Go on and set the book down and give it a shot...I'll wait. I'm not going anywhere.)

Peripheral vision is important for motorcyclists because when we get target fixated we ignore our peripheral vision, and we really can suffer. Target fixation is when you're staring *soooo* intently at something, you become *soooo* targeted on it that you fixate on it—you literally stop seeing all the other things out there. Your eyes stop moving about, you get that focused tunnel vision, and (for me) even stop hearing sounds because you're fully focused on that one thing. The legend goes that dive bomber pilots would often get so fixed on putting bombs on target that they would ride it into the ground before they realized they needed to pull out. True? Maybe—maybe not, but an excellent story—or myth. Either way, when you're engaged in a dangerous activity if you allow yourself to become totally absorbed with one task to the exclusion of gathering relevant peripheral information you can end up in a real bind.

Imagine riding your motorcycle in traffic and having that tunnel vision of target fixation start to happen. You're convinced you're late. You need to be somewhere in ten minutes. It's a fifteen minute ride. Naturally you *think* you're paying more attention 'cause you're really concentrating on working your way through traffic. You're in city traffic, it's not moving really fast, maybe 25, but riding in traffic can be a little like a shooting gallery, you pick off one target and then move to another; pass this sedan, then slip past that van, gotta get past this bus...*good* I can shoot the

gap between the bus and this garbage truck on my right—*cool*
the garbage barge is slowing so I can have some more room—
roll on the throttle, flick into the space—CRAP!!! DOUBLE
PARKED METER MAID CART!

Thump. Skitter. Grind.

Target fixated on shooting the gap, you forgot to process the
peripheral information. What was the peripheral information?
It's a simple issue: *Why* was the garbage truck slowing? It turns
out he was hoping to let you get by and then squeeze into *your*
lane so he could get around the annoying little meter maid cart
that was double parked in *his* lane. Lucky for you he was slowing
enough that stopping isn't a big deal for him, and you don't end
up with a double whammy.

Don't misunderstand me. Intense focus or concentration is a
good thing. I'm going in for some hand surgery in the next few
weeks (trigger finger, look it up), and I absolutely want the guy
who's cutting on me to be completely focused on his job. That
is why there will be so many folks in the room with us; it's not
just me and the surgeon. Even though I will be fully conscious
and there's not much risk, there's gonna be an anesthesiologist
and a surgical nurse (maybe two). Why? Because the surgeon has
enough things to focus on; he needs someone to watch all the
peripherals.

Lots of bad things can happen when you're overly focused
on something. You can lose all the peripheral vision and hit
the meter maid. You can burn the soufflé because you were too
focused on the rib eye. You can forget your spouse's birthday
because it's right in the middle of the holidays and you got all
caught up in decorating the house (yes, it happens). However,
there are good things that can happen when you're overly zeroed
in on something...like what?

Friends. When you're so close to an idea or activity and
you are so completely centered and exclusionary that you have
absolutely no peripheral vision *that's* when friends make a
difference. "Getting another perspective on something" doesn't
necessarily mean leaving the planet and looking at something

from space; it can mean "open your vision." Look around. See the things in the periphery. Friends often recognize we're target fixated and can warn us to get our head up and look around. One of the duties of friends is to help each other—and I don't just mean holding someone's hair up out of the way when they're tossing their cookies in the rest room of the local dive. You may need to be the one, after the third beer who says, "You realize this is gonna end up in the rest room if you don't slow down a little?"

Friends? Allow me to tell you two important things before I head to the can with you to keep your lovely locks out of the vomit and urinal cakes (What? Haven't seen that? You need to get out more; any porcelain in a pinch!). *The* big mistake riders make is to ride like most people drive—staring at the license plate in front of them. We lock our center of vision on that stamped metal plate, and we just follow the one in front of us. Willfully, we blind ourselves to all the vital information that lays just outside our field of vision. Living your life two seconds ahead, with no interest in the world around us, is deadly. Here's a couple tips:

Rule 1. Keep your head and eyes up and moving. Look *around*. Gather information. Don't get target fixated. Remember all that "the more you know" crap? *It's true.* The missing bit of information is the bit that kills you.

Rule 2. If you are focused, you can still gather peripheral information. Remember looking at the word in the center? You can't *read* the ones on the margins but you can *see* them. Once you see them you can flick your center of vision there if you need to and get more information.

Peripheral vision is excellent for alerting you to motion. Use it. Practice using it. The next time you're staring into someone's face and listening intently to the story of how their cat keeps pooping on the bed, take a moment, hold their gaze, and see how much you *can* get with your peripheral. You weren't listening anyway! Try and see what you can see without looking. It's fun. The bottom line is simple though—keep your head on a swivel.

# SAND

Here's the deal: I hate sand. Strike that—I like sand when it's where it's supposed to be, like on the beach. I hate sand when it's where it's not supposed to be.

Sand on beach = Good.

Sand in shorts = Bad.

Sand in your shorts at the beach = Expected. (In fact, at the beach you expect to find sand in all the nooks and crannies of your personal person; you expect it so it's not a big deal, just uncomfortable.)

Finding sand in your shorts when you don't expect it is the tough business. Take when you're working with concrete for example. Concrete has sand in it, and if you're mixing up concrete in a wheelbarrow you need to be careful because you can get that sand on your hands and then transfer it to...other areas.

The thing about sand is that it's often hard to see when you have it on you; you tend to feel it first. The grit, the abrasion, the sense of something on your skin comes first, then you look to see what's there and *voila!* Sand. One of the amazing things about sand is how hard it can be to spot, but how easy it is to feel. Here's another example: ever have sand in your bed? Just a couple of grains? Grrrrrrrr. You—just—have—to—fix—it—NOW! Sand, where it isn't supposed to be is absolutely intolerable and can really surprise and upset you!

Ever find sand—a couple of grains—in your chow? Like in that sandwich at the beach? Should have expected that right? You'll toss the whole sandwich won't you? Sand grinds on your teeth, it *just plain sucks* to find sand in your food.

Sand is insidious, it can hide from you; in great heaping mounds and drifts you can avoid it. It's easy to spot when there's a ton of it. The difficulty comes in the fact that just a little sand, an undetectable amount, can put a motorcycle on its side so fast you end up sliding down the road asking, "What happened?"

You can avoid rocks, pine needles, branches, kangaroos, or socks on the road cause you can see them. Gravel is pretty easy to spot, as are oil slicks, radiator spills, tar snakes, and dead possums. Sand hides, and sometimes the first you know of it is when the front or rear starts sliding. An unexpected slide can be a terrifying thing. If the bike suddenly lets go, an important thing to remember is that the motorcycle slipping doesn't mean you *have* to crash. A big, important part of the equation is how you react to the motorcycle sliding. When the tires slide, do you chop the throttle? Do you jerk the bars back toward you? Grab the brakes? A slipping wheel will often regain traction if you don't suddenly change the physical equation with violent inputs.

Don't freak out—keep riding. When the bike misbehaves, we often react by trying to stop. We chop the throttle, pull in the clutch, hit the brakes, and the bike goes, "WTF are you doing?" Then, overwhelmed with conflicting input all the traction is gone, control is lost, and BANG! you're on the ground. We stop riding and start crashing instead.

Life throws those blind jabs at you, too. For me, it was diabetes. One night I started waking up in the middle of night thirsty as heck and the next thing you know I was shooting insulin. My pancreas just quit working. I never saw that one coming. It was a complete shock. No one in my immediate family was diabetic. When a part of your body just up and quits it's as shocking as having your motorcycle suddenly move to the outside of the turn—you get blind-sided. Diabetes scared the heck out of me. Suddenly I was chronically ill. A small but major organ had quit. Untreated I would die. I was in for a life long dependency on insulin.

Like slipping on sand, I never saw it coming. I just suddenly was diabetic.

Once you've been surprised the question becomes: what am I gonna do about it? Grab the brakes? Chop the throttle? Clutch in? Look down at your hands? Freak out?

Or keep riding?

When the Doctor told me, "You have Type One Diabetes. You're probably going to be injecting insulin the rest of your life," I didn't ignore him, but I didn't jump up, run down, and get counseling. I didn't weep, wail, or gnash my teeth. Doc set me up with a prescription, an appointment with a Diabetic Educator, and gave me a pat on the back, then he sent me home. I laid in bed and thought about my new future—of injections and blood samples and packing "diabetic stuff" with me everywhere. (Did I mention one of the benefits of diabetes? You get sick easier and will stay sick longer—in other words, the flu or a cold can be reeeeally annoying!) Like anyone after an unexpected slide, I went back to see if I could decipher what had happened. I looked through my family history. I tried to think what in the world brought this on. What had I done to deserve this?

The answer was—nobody knows. Could be genetic, could be viral, could be...well it just is; I'm diabetic. Only thing that's for sure is my body produces no insulin. None. Zippo. (Crappy, Icelandic pancreas.)

Next day? The sun rose. I was still diabetic, and I got up and set out on how to be a television news photographer *and* a diabetic. I didn't chop the throttle and stop working, though the thought crossed my mind. I wondered, "Should I take a few days off? You know this is a life changing illness." I decided the thing to do was stay on the throttle. I didn't think of all the things I couldn't do, I just started to figure out how to do the things I had been doing. Diabetes could control me, or I could control my diabetes. I chose to be in charge. Was it scary? Sometimes yes. Did I make mistakes? Yes. But I got back into life and have been able to live the way I want to. Diabetes doesn't own me—I own it. Some days I take five shots a day. Why? Because I'm my own pancreas now and if I eat, I'm in charge.

Getting scared by sand on a motorcycle can be the same way— it can scare the crap out of you, drive you into a nasty crash, even scare you off the bike. *Or* you can stay calm, take control of the situation, keep your eyes up, stay on the gas, and get on with your life. It's OK to be frightened after something bad happens—it's natural. The thing to avoid is letting something bad stop you from doing things that you love.

Does riding through sand mean you'll always fall? Nope, but it can scare you badly. *Oh,* and one other thing: falling isn't guaranteed, but getting up should be.

Since I was diagnosed with diabetes I've had two more children (total 4), worked as a television news photographer, helped get a fledgling television station on air, worked as a local producer/director, changed careers, been teacher of the year at my high school, moved to a small farm, learned to put up hay, raise cattle, become a certified motorcycle instructor, am a Fire Commissioner, have traveled and worked as a camera operator on nationally broadcast sporting events, helped kids get to six state championships in video production, managed to celebrate our twentieth year of marriage, and sent two kids to college.

Am I proud of what I've done since I became "diabetic"? Sure, but really, all I did was keep doing what I wanted. I just kept riding.

My pop (Grandpa Crash) used to say, "Sometimes you can't control what happens to you, all you can control is how your react."

Giving up is never the answer. Know where you want to go, keep your eyes up, and if things get squirrelly stay on the gas— keep riding!

# LEGACY

Mrs. Crash and I were in Kansas City recently and had the opportunity to toodle around the countryside in a rented car seeing the sights. OK, it was a minivan; and yes, I disgust myself—but I had no choice in the matter. When we're "abroad" in a car we carry a GPS, and we have a habit of turning the GPS off and then driving around to wherever seems interesting, and you'd be shocked to know how often we find cool stuff. It's always neat to find a small town with a two-story firehouse that has that painted line twelve feet up that says: "Flood of 1923"; or stumbling into the "Hometown of JC Penny." We like just drivin' around checking things out. We call our GPS "Maggie" and, yes, I talk to her—it just seems right; when she's saying,"Recalculating," I just need to say, "Recalculate *this.*" Or after we've been driving around aimlessly it's nice to turn her back on and say: "Maggie— get me back to the hotel!"

For me, driving around aimlessly is fun. It's empowering to look at a sign with arrows pointing different ways and say: "Weston. That's like Michael Westen from 'Burn Notice'—we're going there!" Yes, I am a TV nerd *and* I like getting lost in the countryside and being rescued by the omniscient Maggie.

As we're driving along, we come to a T in the road. Across the intersection there's a small graveyard and a red brick Baptist church. This is rolling hill country, there's tobacco fields and barns around, the telephone pole next to the church is being claimed by Virginia Creeper (or is it Kudzu?)—some of the roads I've been on are gravel...it's feeling pretty "Cool Hand Luke" and WHAM, there's a teeny little church and graveyard.

Could you resist? There's old headstones, bleached and weeping, no doubt hard to read...who could pass up just taking a peek. I turn in, drive around through the headstones and monuments, and park next to the church under the big tree (sycamore I believe). Someday, we'll do this sort of thing on a motorcycle, but right now we're stuck in a car—we're taking time alone as our five students compete in the SkillsUSA National Championships in Kansas City.

After reading the historical marker on the church (built with bricks made by slaves on site) we go wandering, looking at dates and names. What does all this have to do with motorcycles? Trust me, I'm going somewhere here. I'm looking at a weatherworn marble marker, trying to read a name and date because it looks like a child's marker, and I hear Mrs. Crash calling to me. "Come look at this." She waves me over.

I've been married for twenty-two years. Why? Because if it's important to her, it's important to me, too. Over I go. There's a large granite marker which says:

"Abraham Lincoln's Other Mary, Mary Owens Vineyard 1808-1877, Here Lies Mary Owens Vineyard Who Rejected Abraham Lincoln's Proposal of Marriage in 1837"

Wow. Can you imagine? One hundred and thirty-three years after you're gone—your claim to fame is that you gave Abraham Lincoln the "No...thank you."

How much does that suck? Did she have kids? Was she active in the church Quilting Club? Beloved spouse? Cherished grandmother? Patron of the Arts? Outstanding citizen? Belle of the South? What sort of person was Mary Owens? The sort that turned Abraham Lincoln down.

That's a hard legacy.

Ever think about what's on your *motorcycling* headstone? Squid? Stud? Master? Knucklehead? Mentor? Monkey? When your riding buddies get together and are shooting the shiz, what are they gonna say about you when you're gone? Are you simply another rider? Or are you something more? Sometimes people leave a legacy that we didn't recognize. Take Randy Mamola for example: Champion Roadracer? TV commentator? How about the guy who finished second *four times* back in the days of the wicked two-stroke 500cc Gran Prix motorcycle racing? Yeah, 1980, 1981, 1984 and 1987...second place overall. Always the bridesmaid, never the bride. You could mention that he's one of the most likeable riders out there, and everybody seems to like him, and that he's a great spokesman for the sport, too!

But the temptation is to remember his failings—he could end up Mary Owens Vineyard style—"Finished Second." Yuck.

I'm not too worried about that happening because Mr. Mamola is more than an ex-roadracer; in fact, he's one heck of a decent human being and has a wonderful, impressive legacy; it's called Riders For Health, an organization he helped found that provides transportation to healthcare workers in Africa. When you live in small scattered villages it's tough to get to the doctors—there's not much of a public transportation system and vehicles are unreliable; roads can be poor, and equipment and fuel tough to come by. It turns out there is great way to get doctors or medics into the countryside—motorcycles. Check out Riders for Health on the Web, you'll see how Mr. Mamola has really made a difference in the world. Riders for Health provides training, equipment, and regular maintenance for vehicles that deliver medicine and medics throughout rural Africa.

I've never met Mr. Mamola (although the odds of my meeting him *are* greater than my meeting Mary Owens) but I feel safe in saying that it's clear to me his legacy isn't what "could have been" or "almost was" but what "*is*."

Think about yourself for a moment—what are you gonna be remembered for? Are you going to be remembered for what you almost did? A bad decision? Something you *almost* did? *Or* are you crafting a legacy? Maybe it's time to define yourself so you don't end up with a headstone that says: "Dude *Almost* Was..."

You can find Mary Owens Vineyard in the Pleasant Ridge Cemetery, outside Weston, Missouri, on the P Highway. Randy Mamola? I don't know. Look for motorcycles. He's out and about, if you see him, shake his hand and tell him he's an inspiration; I know I would.

# AFTERWORD

Life's great endeavors often have a way of pushing all things back into the shade. Compiling and fine tuning this manuscript is a great example of how one thing tries to push to the center and hog all the daylight. At the end of 2010 on top of all the usual stuff that takes up our lives I was: taking a 200 level Statistics course, preparing and administering finals to my own students, juggling all of life's usual crap, *and* trying to finish this book.

Things were pretty hectic. Then I received an unexpected phone call from my oldest brother Steve (I've got three—no sisters). My little brother had suffered a subarachnoid hemorrhage and was in the hospital awaiting to be transferred to Stanford University Medical Center for surgery. His condition was critical.

I was a floored. My first immediate reaction to "He's had a brain hemorrhage" was the base fear that he had died; followed by relief when I was told he hadn't, backed up by fear of how much damage may have been done. You've heard the expression "my heart dropped"? Yea, it's true; that short freefall of fear, the catch that it's not the worst, then the return of fear with "How bad?" He was awake, responding to command, and in a great deal of discomfort. All good signs.

Later that night I was on the phone with my mom when she said, "I'm not sure what else to do."

I involuntarily answered, "We'll just keep riding, Mom, we'll just keep riding."

The words just fell out of my mouth. I do truly believe that motorcycling presents us with metaphors for almost all of life's problems. What to do in the face of adversity, of confusion, of fear?—The best advice is the same advice I give riders:

"Just keep riding."

Don't quit. Don't panic. Keep riding. Keep thinking. Keep trying.

The main artery that feeds blood between the right and left halves of my brother's brain had started to leak. It happened while he was in the shower. He woke up on the floor of the shower in intense pain and with numbness in both arms. Precisely at that moment he had to make a decision. Wait? Or Act? He got up, dressed, and went into my mom's house and said, "Take me to the Hospital." He didn't panic. He didn't lay down and take a nap and hope it went away. He didn't lay there and think, "It hurts too much to move."

He got up and kept riding, survived the event, found help, and dealt with the situation. Where will things go from here? Only time will tell.

When my high school students want to quit because a project seems too hard or too muffed up to fix I often say to them: "You're not dead yet—don't stop breathing!" I encourage them to keep fighting. I'll say, "If you think you're dead, keep breathing until you're *sure* you're dead and then keep breathing anyway." I tell them how, when things go wrong for riders, we often just accept the idea that we're going to crash and that guarantees a wreck. Riders, I tell them, just need to remember that when things go wrong, they have to keep riding and not start crashing. Keep riding, I say.

The beauty of motorcycles is that they teach you about life; and life can teach you about motorcycles. You just need to listen.

Keep riding.